BEHOLD A PALE HORSE

World Depopulation

Robert Greyeagle

A sincere thank you is due to my Brother, Daniel Greyeagle who has stood with me throughout time.

CONTENTS

CHAPTER 1: THE ILLUMINATI

"And I looked, and behold, a pale horse! And its rider's name was Death, and Hades followed him. And they were given authority over a fourth of the earth, to kill with sword and with famine and with pestilence and by wild beasts of the earth."
~ Revelation 6:8[1]

T he following is fact.
Or is it fiction?
Weigh the evidence and decide.

You - and I - have a date with Death scheduled by the Elite of this World who rule our governments and economies, countries, and kingdoms.

They go by many names or no name, but one of the oldest and most mysterious is - the "Illuminati"[2].

The "Illuminated" Ones with special, hidden knowledge of power and control. The Enlightened. Different than you and I. Better, so they think.

Today the population of the world - the sum total of all living humans on Earth - is over 7.3 BILLION[3]. That's 7,300,000,000. To understand that number, think of this: if a child were born every minute of every day of every week, every month, and every year - it would take almost 14,000 years to reach that number. Impressive isn't it? The consensus is that the Earth's population surpassed 7 billion on March 12, 2012 and is expected to climb to 10.5 billion by 2050. Only thirty-eight years later.

The Illuminati and the World Elite[4] consider the people of the Earth - men, women, and children - to be "useless eaters[5]" and they have a plan to solve the overabundance of these "cattle.[6]" That plan is to de-populate[7] the world to levels acceptable to them.

They decide, they're in control because they're special.

In Elberton County, Georgia, any local residents know that on a local hilltop exists an unusual granite monument. Known commonly among them as "The Georgia Guidestones" and elsewhere as the "American Stonehenge". The Stones consist of five rough stone slabs that together support a common capstone. They have been engraved in twelve different languages: eight current languages and four ancient/dead tongues. As one moves around the monument, there are inscriptions taking the form of guidelines - some might even say commandments, since there are ten. Are they a link to the Illuminati who work to rule our world?

We can call this monument "mysterious" because of the story of its origin. Its construction cannot be linked to a single individual beyond that of the "disappearing man" who sanctioned it building. In June of 1979, an articulate, well-dressed man visited the office of a local stone mason company to hire them to raise a new monument. Identifying himself as "R. C. Christian". His claimed he spoke for a philanthropic group. Many years later, R. C. Christian is still an unknown.

Who was he really who are the people he supposedly represented?

"In the public library in Elberton, I found a book written by the man who called himself R.C. Christian. I discovered that the monument he commissioned had been erected in recognition of Thomas Paine[8] and the occult philosophy he espoused. Indeed, the Georgia Guidestones are used for occult ceremonies and mystic celebrations to this very day. Tragically, only one religious leader in the area had the courage to speak out against the American Stonehenge, and he has recently relocated his ministry."

The Mysterious Georgia Guidestones In Elberton County, Northern Georgia

ID 31335928 © Sean Pavone | Dreamstime.com

INScriptions:

The carvings on the Georgia Guidestones can be outlined into four areas:

Hegemony, Power, and the formation of a single World Government

Population Control and Restricting Reproduction

Nature, Environment, Conservation and Man's Relationship to these

Mysticism-Spirituality

THE MESSAGE OF THE GEORGIA GUIDESTONES:

• "Maintain humanity under 500,000,000 in perpetual balance with nature."
• "Guide reproduction wisely - improving fitness and diversity."
• "Unite humanity with a living new language."
• "Rule passion - faith - tradition - and all things with tempered reason."
• "Protect people and nations with fair laws and just courts."
• "Let all nations rule internally resolving external disputes in a world court."
• "Avoid petty laws and useless officials."
• "Balance personal rights with social duties."
• "Prize truth - beauty - love - seeking harmony with the infinite."
• "Be not a cancer on the earth - Leave room for nature - Leave room for nature."[9]

It's an interesting list. On the surface many of the points seem warm and friendly, but when thought through to their logical ends, their malevolent nature is exposed.

According to this message, the only acceptable level for the world's population is five hundred million people. 500,000,000! The Earth's human population hasn't been that low since 1500 A.D (some prefer CE or current era). 500 million! That means 6.5 billion (6,500,000,000) people must die to meet this goal. A world with only half a billion people would seem roomy and very comfortable. But, limiting the population of the earth to 500 million would require the elimination of 93% of the world's people! Imagine taking New York City with its current population of approximately 8.3 million and reducing it to 600,000 people! There'd be lots of room! And lots of empty, rotting structures. Or a smaller city like Austin, TX with a population below 700,000 would end with 50,000. An even better visual picture can be seen if you take your local high school with 1000 kids and reduce it to only 70 students!

Out of over 7,300,000,000 people today, where do the other 6,525,000,000 - 6.5 BILLION - go?

The latest proclaimed "environmental crisis" precludes doing this reduction in population over the hundreds of generations it would take, so, it must be done quickly "if the planet is to be saved." Is there more than one relatively quick approach to do this? Maybe only Democide: murdering a people by a government using genocide, politicide, and mass murder.

Establishing a system to resolve "external disputes in a world court" foreshadows the current push to expand the International Criminal Court (ICC) and a World Government through the United Nations. The emphasis in the Guidestones on preserving nature anticipates the radicalism of the environmental movement of the 1990's, and the reference to "seeking harmony with the infinite" is only a foretaste of today's drive to replace Judeo-Christian beliefs with a "New" Spirituality[10].

Sustainable Development and the insistence of its inclusion in all aspects of life also has its place on the Guidestones. Any time the phrase "Sustainable Development[11]" is used, substitute the term "socialism" to be able to understand the intention. And "socialism" translates to "communism" according to Karl Marx. In protests demanding action to stop "global warming" or "climate change", thousands gathered around the USA on September 21, 2014 and they removed their masks. Most of the promoters and participants openly declared their relationship with communism. All of this is about control and power. Control of reproduction, control of world governance. A realignment placing the importance of nature and the environment over Humankind and replacing natural, age-old beliefs with a new, man-made and man-centered spirituality. A move away from the recognition of powers over and above the abilities of Humankind and a rush toward the hubris and narcissism that were the lessons from the Tower of Babel[12].

It has been noted that there is a common theme in the ideas promulgated in the "Earth Charter[13]" and those engraved on the Georgia Guidestones. Could they have shared a similar beginning?

The Earth Charter was developed in 1968 by Maurice Strong and Mikhail Gorbachev, both members of The Club of Rome. This document is "an international declaration of fundamental values and principles considered useful by its supporters for building a just, sustainable, and peaceful global society in the 21st century." It is a list of "values and principle" that must be embraced by the world to achieve a "just society". Using the word "democracy" while advocating unquestioned compliance. Strong, one time Secretary General of the United Nations Conference on the Human Environment, also commissioned a report for the 1972 UN Stockholm conference resulting in "Only One Earth: The Care and Maintenance of a Small Planet" by Barbara Ward and Rene Dubos. This work is said to be the birth of the Sustainable Movement.

So many connections and similarities associate with the message of the Georgia Guidestones.

Some may see these principles and commands etched on the Stones as a positive influence on a future world - why do many view this with distaste and loathing?

Because this structure cries out a warning to us that that there are actually a secret groups determined to rule the world and ..
• Psychopathically and dramatically reduce the population of the world.
• Promote Radical Naturalism as of more import than Humanity.
• Establish a world government with themselves at the head.
• Replace true worship with a man-created, mandatory

"universal" spirituality.[14]

While claiming light they are yet filled with darkness.

Since few Americans - or anyone - know of the existence of the Georgia Guidestones or their inscribed notes to humanity, does this reveal the hand of the Illuminati and their control over media, thoughts, and events?

The Guidestones offer a strong message. Once we've heard the message, then what?

It has been noted that the Georgia Guidestones are a point on earth's Ley Lines of power. This is a grid system that is said cover the earth and is part of Planetary Energetic Grid Theory. Part of the occult Sacred Geometry. Is this a coincidence? Or did the promoters of the Guidestones pick the site bases on these mystical lines of power? And occult connection where there is already deep mystery.

Without any qualms let's just say straight out that there are dark forces behind the Illuminati and other groups like them. Specifically, the force behind the Illuminati has a name and that name is Lucifer. The Illuminati do not worship God the Creator, they worship Lucifer the Fallen Angel, the Rebellious Creature who demanded to be God. He is who they worship in false; it's to him they give allegiance in false fealty. They desire power, but dark power. They want complete control over the lives of every person on earth.

Who are the Illuminati and how did they gain control of governments and economies?

There have been many alignments or "orders" of nations and peoples since the early days after Creation. Each culture expresses their unique views and definitions of the world around them. In past centuries, the more a People were isolated from each other the greater the variance of methods and styles and "order". As interactions and communications have increasingly spanned the globe thanks to ingenuity and technology, many aspects of these cultures have been shared and many have been embraced by disparate Peoples the world over.

In a similar way, governments, alliances, trade, markets...have all interacted more and more in ways that influence each other for better or worse. An example would be the world before the American Revolution. The "World Order" before was one where Royalty and Aristocrats ruled without question over their people and lands. Afterwards was seen a reshaping of national and regional borders, a realignment of powers and the beginning of 200 years of fading Royal Power worldwide. Another example would be the effects of World

War II. Beforehand saw a "World Order" with the last bits of Royalty still holding power and many Empires with large holdings. Afterwards an entirely new World Order emerged. One in which an energetic America rose to prominence, no longer just one of many, the USA became the standard bearer of Democracy, freedom, and capitalism.

When it comes to the emerging New World Order, a majority of Americans are in a sleepwalking state of ignorance. If a majority of people knew and understood the danger - not just coming, but already here - there would be a revolution in the streets tomorrow morning.

If one listens, frequently can be heard statements promising the possibility of an all New World Order around the corner. A realignment of all world powers and peoples.

All that's needed is the right spark.

The puppets who run our governments can be overthrown with their handlers.

Made up of a few elite billionaires who pull the strings and control our so-called leaders; they print money out of thin air only to loan it back to our governments at exorbitant interest rates we are unable to repay. These should be hunted down, arrested, tried, and imprisoned for crimes against common people, against nations and against all humanity.

Our shadow government - the Globalist International Bankers - are responsible for every war involving Americans that has occurred since 1776. They have murdered leaders: Martin Luther King, Jr., Robert F. Kennedy, Malcolm X, Mohandas Gandhi, James Garfield, Huey Long, William McKinley, Yitzhak Rabin, Anwar Sadat, Benazir Bhutto - all acts that directed the course of history. And these Men of Evil assassinated Abraham Lincoln in 1865 and ninety-eight years later, John F. Kennedy in 1963.

The purpose of this book is to open a proverbial "can of worms", to crack the right crypt that will expose the Shadow Government. The individuals who run nations and economies. International Bankers who pull the strings of puppet leaders. The very people whose goal it is to bring about a despotic World Government and the enslavement of uncooperative American citizens in internment camps.

Abraham Lincoln arrived with wife, Mary, in his Studebaker carriage at Ford's Theatre in Washington, D.C., on the evening of April 14th, 1865, to see a performance of the British comedy Our American Cousin. They shared the presidential box with their guests, a young couple, Major Henry Rathbone, and Miss Clara Harris. Mary sat close to her husband, holding his hand. Between 10:15 and 10:30, she spoke to him quietly saying, "What will Miss Harris think of my hanging on to you so?" The president replied, "She won't think anything about it." Those are the last recorded words of Abraham Lincoln. Moments later he was shot and killed.

The assassin was a well-known actor from a prominent family - John Wilkes Booth. After shooting Lincoln, Booth jumped the eleven feet from the balcony down to the stage, breaking his leg. Limping away, he later claimed to have called out, "Sic semper tyrannis" - a Latin phrase meaning "Thus always to tyrants" (the moto for the State of Virginia) - making a connection to the murder of Julius Caesar.

Lincoln lived through the night, attended by his family. He died shortly after 7:00 A.M. in the morning of April 15th.
He was succeeded in office by Vice President Andrew Johnson, a man who reversed many of Lincoln's major accomplishments, in many ways setting back the cause of civil rights for a hundred years.

On April 26th, a search party found Booth and one co-conspirator in a Virginia barn. The companion surrendered only to be later hanged. Booth refused surrender and was understandably, but conveniently shot dead by his apprehenders.

* * *

John F. Kennedy, accompanied by his wife, Jacqueline Bouvier Kennedy, Texas Governor John Connally, and his wife, were traveling in a motorcade through the streets of Dallas, Texas, on November 22, 1963. One more stop on a multi-city tour to build support for his reelection campaign. He was en route to the Dallas Trade Mart where he was scheduled to make a lunch-time speech. At 12:30 P.M., shots rang out; the president, riding in the back seat of a Lincoln Continental four-door convertible, was hit in the neck and head. He was rushed to a nearby hospital where he died at 1:00 P.M. He had never regained consciousness. The nation's loss was immediately felt, as television and radio stations broadcast the message that Kennedy had been shot and killed. He was succeeded by Vice President Lyndon Baines Johnson (1908-1973), who took the oath of office aboard an airplane just after 2:30 P.M. Later that day Lee Harvey Oswald (1939-1963) was arrested as the suspected assassin of Kennedy. On November 24th while in police custody, Oswald was murdered by night club owner Jack Ruby. Ruby's birth name was Rubenstein. In 1964 the Warren Commission, a government committee authorized to investigate the assassination, determined that Oswald acted alone in killing Kennedy. Many critics, including myself, still question the Commissions' conclusions, contending that Oswald was part of a larger conspiracy.

The purpose of this book is to open a proverbial "can of worms", to crack the right crypt that will expose the Shadow Government. The individuals who run nations and economies. International Bankers who pull the strings of puppet leaders. The very people whose goal it is to bring about a World Government and the enslavement of uncooperative American citizens in internment camps built by FEMA. These camps exist now throughout the United States. Research it for yourself. It's easy to check.

So, just exactly who and what are the Illuminati?

Secretly subverting the United States and its Constitution is a small group of men whose sole objective is to enslave humanity in a satanic plot for a one world government. To give a very clear picture of this plot, let's go back to its beginning, the middle of the 18th Century, and name the men who put that plot into action.

The plot to control all the world can be seen in the actions taken in the 1760's to bring about the organized by Adam Weishaupt of the secret society, the Illuminati on May 1, 1776.

A Luciferian conspiracy

Adam Weishaupt was a convert to Catholicism and later became a Jesuit-trained catholic priest and a professor of Canon Law at Inglecot University. In 1770 he rejected Christianity for some unknown reason. He left the Catholic Church, embraced the Devil's conspiracy, and organized the Illuminati. He wrote a master plan that was to give the Synagogue of Satan, an oligarchy of Financiers domination to impose their ideology on the remains of the human race.

The purpose of the Illuminati conspiracy is the destruction of the Catholic Church and all religions and the founding of a one-world dictatorship[15]. Weishaupt set up the Illuminati "to terrorize the populace into the acceptance of its rule." Influencing all war, thereafter, beginning with the French Revolution, has been promoted by the Illuminati under various monikers and guises. After the Illuminati was exposed and gained notoriety,Weishaupt and his co-conspirators changed their tactics and began using many names and became covert.

The name "Illuminati" seals the connection. Weishaupt himself said the word is derived from Lucifer meaning "holders of the light". "And no wonder! For Satan himself transforms himself into an angel of light."[16]

Weishaupt completed the formation of the Illuminati on May 1, 1776. Communist nations observe yearly celebrations on May 1st. It is "International Workers' Day". Is this in honor of this infamous event?

Weishaupt's plan required the destruction of all governments and religions. The objective would see the dividing of all peoples into enemy camps based on political, economic, social, cultural, ideological, sexual, and other divisors. Exactly the conditions we are experiencing in the United States now. Opposing sides would be armed and mobilized and goaded into incidents causing war and destruction. They would be encouraged to fight - to weaken themselves - gradually destroying national governments and religious influences.

The plan of operation:

Weishaupt's plan directed his Illuminati to take the following actions to accomplish their goals.

Financial and sexual bribery and extortion to be used to control men in high places in governments and other influential fields. Once prominent persons had fallen for the lies, deceits, lusts, and temptations of the Illuminati, they were to be held in bondage by application of political and other forms of blackmail, threats of financial ruin, public exposure, and physical harm. Even death to themselves and loved members of their families.

The Illuminati who were on the faculty of colleges and universities were to cultivate students possessing exceptional mental ability and who belonged to well-bred families with international leanings and recommend them for special training in Internationalism. Such training was to be provided by granting scholarships, like the Rhodes scholarship, to those selected by the Illuminati. All such scholars were to be first persuaded and then convinced that men of special talent and brains had the "right" to rule those "less gifted" on the grounds that the masses do not know what is best for them physically, mentally, or spiritually.

All influential people who were trapped to come under the control of the Illuminati, plus the students who had been specially educated and trained, were to be used as agents and placed behind the scenes of all governments as experts and specialists. They would advise the top executives to adopt policies which would, in the long run, serve the secret plans of the Illuminati one world conspiracy, and bring about the destruction of the governments and religions they were elected or appointed to serve.

They were to obtain absolute control of the press so that all news and information could be slanted to convince the masses that a one world government is the only solution to our many and varied problems. Today that includes all the national radio, TV, and Internet outlets.

After reading these four points of strategy, we have to admit that our mass communications media is controlled at all levels, and that our governments are also infiltrated and controlled. Just like Weishaupt had planned back in the 1700's. Unfortunately, few people are aware of this fact, which is why they make little sense out of many of the world events that take place today.

Let us now go back to the first days of the Illuminati.

Because Britain and France were the two greatest world powers in the late years of the 18th Century, Weishaupt ordered the Illuminati to foment the colonial wars, including the Revolutionary War in America, to weaken the British Empire. They were also ordered to organize the French Revolution in order to destroy the French Empire.

Is all this really possible?

Weishaupt scheduled the French Revolution to start in 1789. However, in 1784, a true act of God placed the Bavarian Government in possession of evidence which proved the existence and intentions of the Illuminati. And that evidence could have saved France if the French Government had not refused to believe it.

An act of God?

Some call it an act of God? Weishaupt had spread his design for the French Revolution beginning in 1784. These had been written into book form, published and sent to all the conspirators in France. The story goes that the French Illuminati, Robespierre, was directed by Weishaupt to aggravate and irritate and terrorize the people of France in such a way to cause unease and bring about revolution. One currier as he rode on his way from Germany to France. was struck and killed - yes - by lightning! Local officials found Weishaupt's plan in the rider's belongings. The Bavarian Government obtained these and after study they ordered a raid of all Weishaupt's properties, homes, and the homes of his associates. The authorities became convinced that the plot real and represented a genuine conspiracy created by the Illuminati. The Illuminati planned to use wars and revolutions to bring about their goals. Bavaria became believers. They outlawed the Illuminati in 1785 and closed all lodges. Bavaria published all the details of the conspiracy a year later. These papers were originally named "The Original Writings of the Order and Sect of the Illuminati". Copies were sent to all Church and State leaders in Europe. This warning went unheeded. Some say due to the power and influence of the Illuminati. The Illuminati went permanently underground.

At the same time, Weishaupt ordered Illuminates to infiltrate into the lodges of Blue Masonry and form their own secret societies within all secret societies. Only Masons who proved themselves internationalists, and those whose conduct proved they had defected from God, were initiated into the Illuminati.

In order to infiltrate into Masonic Lodges in Britain, Weishaupt invited John Robison over to Europe. Robison was a high degree Mason in the Scottish Rite. He was a professor of natural philosophy at Edinburgh University and secretary of The Royal Society of Edinburgh. Robison did not fall for the lie that the objective of the Illuminati was to create a benevolent dictatorship, but he kept his reaction to himself so well that he was entrusted with a copy of Weishaupt's revised conspiracy for study and safekeeping.

Because the warnings about the Illuminati were ignored, the Revolution broke out in 1789, as scheduled by Weishaupt. In order to alert other governments to their danger, Robison published, in 1789, "Proof of a Conspiracy to Destroy All Governments and Religions", but his warnings were ignored.

The Napoleonic Wars:
They directed the French Revolution and then plotted and organized the Napoleonic Wars to topple European Crowned Heads. One group of the Financiers supported Napoleon, another branch financed Britain, Germany, and others. These groups got their impetus from the Illuminati.

After the Napoleonic Wars, the Illuminati wanted all nations to be desperate and so weary of war so they would accept any solution. The Congress of Vienna[17] was created by the puppets of the Illuminati. Here they tried to create something similar to the eventual League of Nations. A first attempt at One World Government. They were confident that all Crowned heads of Europe were so deeply in debt to them they would serve as their stooges. Either willingly or not. The Czar of Russia caught on to this plot and put a stop to it. The Financiers vowed to destroy the Czar and his entire family. This was later accomplished. The Illuminati was not intended to run on a short-term plan. Unlike a conspiracy with expectations of achieving its objective during one man's1 lifetime. The Illuminati operate on the very long-term schedule, whether decades or centuries, they have dedicated themselves and their descendants to achieve the conspiracy. The disaster of the Congress of Vienna led by the Czar of Russia did not end the Illuminati conspiracy, but it did force into a new strategy. Realizing that the moment was yet, the Illuminati decided that, to for the sake of power, they would tighten control of the money system of European nations.

To control the economy:
The Financiers had spread a story that Napoleon had won the Battle of Waterloo, which brought about a stock market panic in England. Stocks had plunged to nothing. International Bankers then bought all the "worthless" stocks for virtually a penny on the dollar, giving them complete control of the economies of Britain and of all Europe. Immediately after the congress held in Vienna, the International Bankers forced Britain to set up a New Bank of England, with them in control. They are in still control today.

Weishaupt died in 1830, before his death, he revised the age-old conspiracy of the Illuminati, which was to organize, finance, direct, and control all international organizations by working agents into executive positions.

The revolutionary program:
Karl Marx created his "Communist Manifesto", under the direction of the Illuminati, while Karl Ritter of Frankfurt University wrote its anti-thesis, also under the direction of the Illuminati. The idea was that those who direct the overall conspiracy could use the contradictions of these two ideologies to enable them to divide larger and larger numbers of the human race into opposing camps, so that they could be armed and brainwashed into fighting and destroying each other,

and all political and religious institutions. Friedrich Nietzsche continued the work Ritter started and helped to develop Racism and then Naziism, which was used to foment World War I and II.

Giuseppe Mazzini, was selected in 1834 by the Illuminati to direct their worldwide revolutionary program, serving in capacity until his death in 1872. Before he died, Mazzini had enticed an American general named Albert Pike[18] into the Illuminati. Fascinated by the idea of a one world government Pike became the head of this conspiracy. Between 1859 and 1871, Pike worked out a long-term military plan for three world wars and many revolutions throughout the world he thought would best forward the conspiracy to its final phase.

CHAPTER 2:
ONE WORLD
GOVERNMENT -
WORLD WARS

The effort of the First World War was to enable the destruction of the Czars in Russia - an act vowed by the International Bankers after the events of Czar Alexander and the Congress of Vienna - and to transform Russia into a fortress of atheism and Communism. Using the fire of animosity stoked by agents of the Illuminati between the German and British Empires to encourage war. Afterwards, Communism would destroy other target governments and weaken their spiritual underpinnings.

A Second War, if needed, would be pushed between the fascist and Zionists. International Communism would be nurtured to a size and strength equal to the challenge of all the Christian World. After reaching that milestone, it would be contained until needed for the final solution.

A Third World War will be caused by using the frictions between political Zionists and the leaders of the Muslim world. Directed in an approach that would have all of Islam and Zionism - Israel - destroy each other. The remaining nations, divided on the issues, will fight amongst themselves to exhaustion - physically, mentally, spiritually, and economically. That will set the stage for the installation of one world government.

A One World Government:
In the final phases of the conspiracy, a one world government is to consist of a dictator - maybe the head of the United Nations, or the Council on Foreign Relations (the Illuminati group in the U.S.), or maybe one of a few billionaires, or the Communists, or one of a select group of scientists. The Dictator would come from a group of Illuminati conspirators who have proven their devotion. All other peoples are to be collected into a "vast conglomeration of monopolized humanity", becoming total slaves of the conspiracy. After WW1, the Illuminati set up in the United States the "Council on Foreign Relations, commonly referred to as the CFR. This CFR is actually the Illuminati now operating in the U.S. Its hierarchy, the mastermind control of the CFR, to a very great extent are descendants of the original Illuminati conspirators, even though many of them have changed their names to conceal this fact[19]."

England has its own version of the CFR, the "British Institute of International Affairs". France, Germany, and other nations, also have the Illuminati operating in this way within their borders. All of these organizations are continuously creating other front organizations to enable infiltration into every phase of the public affairs.

Masterminded and controlled by the Illuminati. - These thoughts and words come from Myron Fagan, who I consider a mentor in my research of the Illuminati, along with Alex Jones and David Icke[20].

Americans don't realize that their country was founded by Freemasons who drafted the US Constitution and Declaration of Independence. Paul Revere, George Washington and most of his generals were Masons. The Freemasons provided Americans still valid ideas - civil liberties, equal opportunity, and no taxation without representation, but they were enticements designed to win power. As you might have noticed, these promises are not being kept.

Most historians won't tell you this, but one did reveal the truth. Bernard Fay[21] (1893-1978) was a Harvard educated Frenchman and is considered an "anti-Mason" due to his 1935 book "Revolution and Freemasonry 1680-1800". It is one of the very few to describe the extent of Masonic participation in the US and French Revolutions. Fay explains that in the 1770's, the US consisted of 13 isolated colonies with different governments, religious affiliations, customs, racial profiles, and social and political structures. There were intense rivalries and longstanding antagonisms. A letter took three weeks to get from Georgia to Massachusetts. Fay wrote, "Masonry alone undertook to lay the foundation for national unity in America because, as a secret society, it could spread throughout the colonies and work steadily and silently. It created in a limited but very prominent class of people a feeling of

American unity without which there would have been no United States". In 1760, there was no town, big or small, where Masonry had not spun its web. Everywhere it was preaching fraternity and unity.

Did you Know...?
- Benjamin Franklin was the Grand Master of a French Lodge, raised millions of Francs to finance Washington's army, and established a chain of Masonic newspapers in all the colonies.[22]

- George Washington was a devoted Mason[23]. After recapturing Philadelphia, he led a parade on Dec. 27, 1778 where he was dressed in full Masonic attire. Fay writes: All the staff officers Washington trusted were Mason, and all leading generals of the army were Masons. They all gathered around their Master Mason Washington and they all met at the 'Temple of Virtue,' a rude structure forming an oblong square forty by sixty feet, one story in height, a single entry which was flanked by two pillars. The atmosphere which surrounded Washington was Masonic and it may be said that the framework of his mind was Masonic.

Fay describes the amount of coordination between Masons in the US and British armies[24]. "Even likely that the unforgettable and mysterious laxness of certain English military campaigns in America, particularly those of the Howe brothers, was deliberate and due to the Masonic desire of the English to reach a peaceful settlement."

Jonathan Williams wrote in 1781 in "Legions of Satan", of the deceptive takeover by the Crown where it's religion will be injected without even being noticed by the people and he that less than two hundred years would pass until the entire nation would be working for a world government under the invisible all-seeing eye[25]. The all-seeing eye on the US dollar bill is a Masonic symbol, put there by Franklin D. Roosevelt, a Mason.

Affiliated Illuminati Groups
The Bilderbergers: Bilderberg is an annual event where influential globalists from Europe and America get together and discuss plans that to coordinate world events such as global taxes or an economic depression that will benefit the New World Order agenda. In 1954, the Bilderberg Group was formed by a Polish political adviser Józef Retinger, who is one of the early advocates of a European Union and a proponent of the Council of Europe. Retinger is widely believed to have been a member of the Vatican and the Knights of Malta. Moat guests to Bilderberg come from presidents, prime ministers, politicians, central bankers, defense experts, royalty, mainstream and Internet media moguls from the West. Past guests have included the likes of Fed Chairman Ben Bernanke, Hank Paulson, David Rockefeller, Henry Kissinger, Timothy Geithner, Condoleezza Rice, Google CEO Eric Schmidt, Madeline Albright and numerous other Trilateral Commission and CFR members.

Jim Tucker, Bilderberg Investigator, said that in 2008 the meetings dealt with implantable microchips to be used as a credit card and an identification device. The micro-chipping of humans on a mass scale. This would be introduced in the guise of fighting terrorism. Homeland Security's current fight against Islamic terrorism has morphed into a fight against domestic extremism. Groups and activists against the government are now being called potential terrorist and extremists by Homeland Security. A microchip could be used to squelch dissent. The complacent would be allowed to travel freely on airplanes as long as they have their microchip able to be compared with information stored in a database elsewhere. This creates a major dilemma for Christians. Taking the chip would allow you will be able to buy and sell to feed your family; however, taking the chip might align you with the anti-Christ. Refusing the chip prevents your ability to buy or sell. You might be killed. Those who align themselves with the anti-Christ will spend eternity in hell.

Bilderberg conferences have consisted of people like George Bush, Sr., George Bush Jr., Hillary Clinton, Barack Obama, James Steinberg, Dick Chaney, Timothy Geithner, the World Bank President, European Commission head, Queen Sofia of Spain and Queen Beatrix of the Netherlands and many others. Journalists Daniel Estulin and Jim Tucker have sources inside the Bilderberg group. Jim Tucker reported that regular attendee Carl Bildt made a speech advocating turning the World Health Organization into a World Department of Health, advocating turning the IMF into a world Department of Treasury, both of course under the auspices of the United Nations. Tucker states this is a giant leap towards World Government. Tucker said Bilderberg members will stress to the public that the problem of global economic crisis and a global pandemic will be the justification for the centralization of power. Daniel Estulin's sources say that Bilderberg plans a prolonged, agonizing depression that dooms the world to decades of stagnation, decline and poverty or an intense-but-shorter depression that paves the way for a new sustainable economic world order, with less sovereignty but more efficiency. Tucker agrees saying that Treasury Secretary Geithner and Carl Bildt touted a shorter recession not a 10-year recession partly because a 10-year recession would damage Bilderberg industrialists themselves, as much as they want to have a global department of labor and a global department of treasury, they still like making money and such a long recession would cost them big bucks industrially because nobody is buying their toys. The tilt is towards keeping it short. Estulin predicted that the housing crash and the 2008 financial meltdown was a result of what the Bilderberg was planning at the 2006 meeting in Canada, and the 2007 conference in Turkey. Estulin's Bilderberg insider-source got this information from pre-meeting booklets which were handed out to Bilderberg members. Estulin warns that the Bilderberg is fostering a false sense of recovery of the economy, suckering investors to plunge back into the stock market to only unleash another massive downturn which will create —massive losses and searing financial pain in the months ahead.

Jim Tucker said Bilderberg also discussed the emergence of a global carbon tax which will be paid directly to the United Nations. Tucker said it will be introduced to the public gradually such as a barely noticeable tax at the gas pump, which will later be increased once it has been established.

Another topic that Estulin points out that Bilderberg will push for the enactment of the Lisbon Treaty, a key centerpiece of the agenda to complete the European Union. The Irish will most likely be coaxed to vote yes on the treaty even though they were very successful in rejecting the first treaty. Tucker's sources say Bilderberg were planning to privately send representatives to Ireland to talk to political leaders in an effort to push the treaty through. Estulin writes that the Bilderberg will also try to neutralize the anti-Lisbon treaty movement called Libertas led by Declan Ganley. One of the Bilderberger's planned moves is to use a whispering campaign in the US media suggested that Ganley is being funded by arms dealers in the US linked to the US military.‖ Note: Ireland now belongs to the EU.

Tucker said the key component of this year's Bilderberg meeting was an effort to get President Obama to slip through ratification of the International Criminal Court treaty, by forwarding it to the Senate to be voted on. Another global treaty Obama has promised he would introduce to the Senate is the global gun-control treaty called CIFTA (The Inter-American Convention against Illicit Manufacturing of and Trafficking in Firearms). To pass the International Criminal Court treaty their tactic is to have Obama is to convince the left-wing Democrats in Congress who really want the International Criminal Court treaty say don't worry, we'll have more liberals in the Senate after the elections so when the new Senate is seated you can ratify it late on a Saturday night when it's too late for Sunday morning papers and to re-plan the Sunday talk shows....there will be no political reprisals.

Bilderberg chairman Étienne Davignon admitted that the Bilderberg helped create the Euro currency in the 1990's. However, leaked documents from the 1955 Bilderberg conference held in Germany had already discussed the creation of the Euro, and the formation of the European Union. There are only a few journalists that are covering Bilderberg's clandestine events[26]. The mainstream media has been locked-out from covering most events. One local journalist who spoke with London Daily News said, "We have been told by senior government officials that covering the events could cost us our jobs." One journalist has been arrested for trying to take a picture of the Hotel at which Bilderberg members resided. Charlie Skelton a writer for the London Guardian has been covering the conference has been arrested for taking pictures of the ocean near the hotel where some members stayed. Officers told Skelton to delete his photos and tried to take his camera; they searched his possessions and later he was detained for the second time immediately before appearing on the Alex Jones radio show. Another journalist group was arrested for taking photographs near the Hotel. Jim Tucker concludes that the global elite are very grim-faced at this year's Bilderberg[27] meeting. He says: "Things are going bad for them, Americans are responding, Europeans are responding, and their program is being blocked."

The treasonous agenda of the Trilateral Commission was published by Devvy Kidd. Devvy Kidd authored the booklets "Why a Bankrupt America" and "Blind Loyalty"; 2 million copies distributed. She left the Republican Party in 1996 and has been an independent voter ever since. Visit Devvy's website at: www.devvy.com. You may also sign up for her free e-mail alerts. The technocratic era involves the gradual appearance of a more controlled society. Such a society would be dominated by the elite, unrestrained by traditional values. "Zbigniew Brzezinski, National Security Adviser to Jimmy Carter and President Bush as co-chairman of the Bush National Security Advisory Task Force; executive director of the Trilateral Commission. My column last week focused on their anti-American agenda. This treasonous operation is another one of the tentacles birthed by the elitists out to destroy our constitutional republic, turn us into a democracy (America is not a Democracy!) and eventually merge all nations into a one world government." said Devvy.

This is real. It is not a conspiracy theory. It is a heinous agenda that is all but complete except for the passage of CAFTA (Central American Free Trade Agreement), FTAA (Free Trade Area of the Americas) and nullification of the Second Amendment. If Bush gets his way and CAFTA and FTAA are ratified, you will see another gigantic sucking sound of millions more American jobs going south of the Hemisphere. So far, Utah appears to be the only state to recognize the danger of this destructive treaty (FTAA).

Few Americans really understood back in 1993 what would happen under GATT because few ever heard of it. Too many simply bought the propaganda from politicians and the rest were more interested in sports, porn, drugs, booze, or partying. Guess how many members of the entire Congress read GATT? Only one - former Sen. Hank Brown. He's the only senator who read this 28,000-page treaty and stated emphatically that no way would he vote for it. Yet, the rest of the Senate ratified this insidious treaty without ever reading it. Sadly, the American people continue electing these same sellouts back into office.

During the hearings on this monster, French financier, the late Sir James Goldsmith, testified in front of the Ernest Hollings committee. He demonstrated that GATT would gut the American textile market. The following are some quotes from the Washington Times, Dec. 6, 1993, which accurately reflect Sir Goldsmith's statements during the hearings: Global free trade will force the poor of the rich countries to subsidize the rich in poor countries. What GATT means is that our national wealth, accumulated over centuries, will be transferred from a developed country like Britain to developing countries like Communist China, now building its first ocean going navy in 500 years. China, with its 1.2 billion people, three Indochinese states with 900 million, the former Soviet republics with some 300 million, and many more can supply skilled labor for a fraction of Western costs. Five dollars in Communist China is the equivalent of a $100 wage in Europe. It is quite amazing that GATT (General Agreement on Tariffs and Trade) is sowing the seeds for global social upheaval and that it is not even the subject of debate in America ... If the masses understood the truth about GATT, there would be blood in the streets of many capitals. A healthy national economy has to produce a large part of its own needs. It cannot simply import what it needs and use its labor force to provide services for other countries. We have to rethink from top to bottom why we have elevated global free trade to the status of sacred cow, or moral dogma. It is a fatally flawed concept that will impoverish and destabilize the industrialized world while cruelly ravaging the Third World.

On June 9, 2005, the House voted 338-86 to reject a motion to withdraw congressional approval of the 1994 agreement establishing the Geneva-based trading body (GATT-WTO). Every Congress-critter who voted to stay in this anti-American, new world order operation must be thrown out of office for continuing to abrogate our sovereignty to foreign countries.

The Trilateral Commission[28] is another little-known entity that is diligently and methodically working to destroy the sovereignty of this nation and put the United States under foreign rule – it is the twin monster of the CFR. Barry Goldwater was one of the lone voices decades ago trying to warn the American people about this operation. He said of the Trilateral Commission: "The Trilateral Commission is international and is intended to be the vehicle for multinational consolidation of the commercial and banking interests by seizing control of the political government of the United States. The Trilateral Commission represents a skillful, coordinated effort to seize control and consolidate the four centers of power – political, monetary, intellectual and ecclesiastical."

It is imperative to look at the companies and institutions these individuals belong to and then one can begin to connect the dots as to why Congress refuses to abolish the unconstitutional, privately owned Federal Reserve, immediately withdraw from the United Nations and the continuing passage of these devastating trade treaties.

Our Republic is perilously close to being destroyed. This isn't about Republican vs. Democrat or any of these other distractions – it's an American issue.

Without question, this factual information is very disturbing to Americans; however, this is about remaining a free and sovereign nation and not falling to communist domination under a world government. William Wallace was depicted saying in the movie, "Braveheart", "What will you do without freedom?" I ask you, the reader, the same.

As previously noted in "Pawns of the Global Elite",

Barack Obama was groomed for the presidency by key members of the Trilateral Commission. Most notably, it was Zbigniew Brzezinski, co-founder of the Trilateral Commission with David Rockefeller in 1973, who was Obama's principal foreign policy adviser. Election attention on Obama was reminiscent of Brzezinski's tutoring of Jimmy Carter prior to Carter's landslide election in 1976.

For anyone who doubts the Commission's continuing influence on Obama, consider that he has already appointed no less than eleven members of the Commission to top-level and key positions in his Administration. According to official Trilateral Commission membership lists, there are only 87 members from the United States (the other 337 members are from other regions). Thus, in less than two weeks since his inauguration, Obama's appointments encompass more than 12% of Commission's entire U.S. membership.

About The Trilateral Commission:
The Trilateral Commission sprang from the Bilderbergers when one of its principal members, Esso or Standard Oil's David Rockefeller came into conflict with his fellows over whether to include Japan in the club. Upon reading the 1970 book "Between Two Ages", David Rockefeller lured its writer, Professor Zbigniew Brzezinski, away from Columbia University to become the Chairman and co-founder of the Trilateral Commission in 1973. Brzezinski, who later became the mastermind of Jimmy Carter's foreign affairs and national security blunders, is still looked to as a policy guru

by the liberal media today. Using the same collectivist mindset, objectives and premise as the CFR, Rockefeller funded and set up the New York-based Trilateral Commission with Zbigniew Brzezinski as its intellectual architect and purposely patterned after Brzezinski's book.

Along with Zbigniew Brzezinski and a few others, including the Brookings Institution, Council on Foreign Relations and the Ford Foundation, Rockefeller convened initial meetings and held their first executive committee meeting in Tokyo in October 1973. Members include corporate CEOs, politicians of all major parties, distinguished academics, university presidents, labor union leaders and not-for-profits involved in overseas philanthropy. The Trilateral Commission was founded to become a type of international CFR. The goal of the Trilateral Commission is to align the free world with the advanced communist states to organize a world government.

CHAPTER 3: CONSPIRATORS

The Trilateral Commission[29] first established in 1973, was founded and funded by international financier, David Rockefeller[30], chairman of the Rockefeller family-dominated Chase Manhattan Bank and Chairman of the Council on Foreign Relations at that time. He was the undisputed king of his family's global corporate empire.

Rockefeller's idea for establishing the commission emerged after he had read the book, "Between Two Ages", by a globalist and establishment scholar, Prof. Zbigniew Brzezinski of Columbia University.

Brzezinski proposed an expansive alliance between North America, Western Europe, and Japan. He suggested that changes in the world necessitated this alliance. "Resist as it might, the American system is compelled gradually to accommodate itself to this emerging international context, with the U.S. government called upon to negotiate, to guarantee and, to some extent, to protect the various arrangements that have been contrived even by private business." Brzezinski wrote.

In his mind, it was necessary for the international

upper class to band together to protect its interests, and to ensure that political leaders in the 1st World Nations were brought to power who would ensure the global financial interests of the Rockefellers and the other ruling elites over those of the majority.

The Trilateral Commission is widely seen as a counterpart to the Council on Foreign Relations. Speaking at the Chase Manhattan International Financial Forums in London, Brussels, Montreal, and Paris, Rockefeller proposed the creation of an International Commission of Peace and Prosperity in early 1972 (which later became the Trilateral Commission). At the 1972 Bilderberg meeting, the idea was widely accepted, but elsewhere, it got a cool reception. According to Rockefeller, the organization could "be of help to government by providing measured judgment."

In July 1972, Rockefeller called his first meeting at Rockefeller's Pocantico compound in New York's Hudson Valley. It was attended by about 250 carefully selected and screened individuals representing the very elite of finance and industry.

William Blasé said about the Council on Foreign Relations[31], "for those confused by the controversies surrounding the New World Order, One World Government, and American concern over giving the UN more power; those unaware of the issues involved; and those wishing more background, I offer the following: Originally presented for an Honors Class "Dilemmas of War and Peace" at New Mexico State University, the paper was ridiculed and characterized by Dr. Yosef Lapid, (an acknowledged and locally quoted "expert" on Terrorism and Middle Eastern affairs) as "paranoid... possibly a symptom of mental illness." Judge for yourself.

Citing source data is the scientific method but does not seem to apply to Conspiracy Theories. A thousand sources may be quoted, yet will not convince the skeptics, the realists. It seems to me the symptoms of mental illness are on their side, if they refuse to look at evidence (There are none so blind as those who WILL not see); or perhaps something more sinister is at work, such as a knowledge of the truth, that does not want YOU to know.

Being paranoid means you believe in delusions of danger, of persecution. If the danger is real and credible it cannot be delusional. Ignoring the evidence hoping that it cannot be true, is more signs of mental illness. It is much more than a difference of philosophy or politics. Raised during the Cold War, we were taught that those who attempted to abolish our national sovereignty and overthrow our Constitutional government were committing acts of treason.

"If one group is effectively in control of national governments and multinational corporations, promotes world government through control of media, foundation grants, and education, and controls and guides the issues of the day, then they control most options available." The Council on Foreign Relations (CFR) has done all these things and has promoted a New World Order for over seventy years. "The CFR is the promotional arm of the Ruling Elite in the United States of America. Influential politicians, academics and media personalities are members. Its experts write scholarly pieces for decision making, the academics expound on the wisdom of a united world, and the media members propagandize the message.

Understanding how these influential people in America became of an organization working purposefully to overthrow the Constitution and American sovereignty, will need to go back to the early 1900's. Felix Frankfurter, Justice of the Supreme Court (1939-1962), said: "The real rulers in Washington are invisible and exercise power from behind the scenes." In a letter to an associate dated November 21, 1933, President Franklin Roosevelt wrote: "The real truth of the matter is, as you and I know, that a financial element in the large centers has owned the government ever since the days of Andrew Jackson." February 23, 1954, Senator William Jenner warned in a speech: "Outwardly we have a Constitutional government. We have operating within our government and political system another body representing another form of government, a bureaucratic elite that believes our Constitution is outmoded." Baron M.A. Rothschild wrote, "Give me control over a nation's currency and I care not who makes its laws."

What is needed to control a government is control over the nation's money. A central bank - like the Federal Reserve - with a monopoly over the supply of money and credit. This had been done in Western Europe, who've created privately owned central banks like the Bank of England.

Mentor to Bill Clinton and Georgetown professor Dr. Carroll Quigley said about the goals of the investment bankers who control central banks: "... nothing less than to create a world system of financial control in private hands able to dominate the political system of each country and the economy of the world as a whole... controlled in a feudalist fashion by the central banks of the world acting in concert, by secret agreements arrived at in frequent private meetings and conferences."

An early attempt at an American central bank, The Bank of the United States (1816-36), was abolished by President Andrew Jackson. He believed it threatened the nation. He wrote: "The bold effort the present bank had made to control the government, the distress it had wantonly produced...are but premonitions of the fate that awaits the American people should they be deluded into a perpetuation of this institution or the establishment of another like it."

Thomas Jefferson wrote: "The Central Bank is an institution of the most deadly hostility existing against the principles and form of our Constitution...if the American people allow private banks to control the issuance of their currency, first by inflation and then by deflation, the banks and corporations that will grow up around them will deprive the people of all their property until their children will wake up homeless on the continent their fathers conquered."

Does this describe the situation in America today?

The U.S. was without a central bank until early in the 20th century when, said Charles Lindbergh, Sr., "The Money Trust caused the 1907 panic, and thereby forced Congress to create a National Monetary Commission." Headed by Senator Nelson Aldrich, John D. Rockefeller, Jr.'s father-in-law, the Commission recommended a central bank.

"The Congress shall have Power....to coin Money, regulate the Value thereof..." (Article I, Section 8, U.S. Constitution) the Federal Reserve Act[32] was passed in December 1913, though unconstitutional, supposedly to stabilize the economy and more financial panics. As Lindberg warned Congress: "This act establishes the most gigantic trust on earth...the invisible government by the money power, proven to exist by the Money Trust investigation, will be legalized." The Great Depression and numerous recessions later, it is obvious the Federal Reserve produces inflation and debt whenever needed, but not stability.

Congressman Louis McFadden, House Committee on Banking and Currency Chairman (1920-31), stated: "When the Federal Reserve Act was passed, the people of these United States did not perceive that a world banking system was being set up here. A super-state controlled by international bankers and industrialists...acting together to enslave the world...Every effort has been made by the Fed to conceal its powers, but the truth is--the Fed has usurped the government." Although named "Federal," the Federal Reserve System is privately owned by member banks, makes its own policies, and is not subject to oversight by Congress or the President. As the overseer and supplier of "money", the Fed gave the banks access to public funds, which increased their lending capacity.

In "Economic Solutions", Peter Kershaw lists the ten major shareholders of the Federal Reserve Bank System: Rothschild: London and Berlin; Lazard Bros: Paris; Israel Seiff: Italy; Kuhn-Loeb Company: Germany; Warburg: Hamburg and Amsterdam; Lehman Bros: New York; Goldman and Sachs: New York; Rockefeller: New York. It is interesting that most of these families just happen to be Jewish. "Why a Bankrupt America," by Devvy Kidd's, says the Federal Reserve pays the Bureau of Engraving & Printing approximately $23 for each 1,000 notes printed - of any denomination. Ten Thousand $100 notes (one million dollars) would cost the Fed $230. They then get a pledge of collateral equal to the face value from the U.S. government. The collateral is our land, labor, and assets - collected by their agents, the IRS. By authorizing the Fed to regulate and create money - and inflation - Congress gave private banks power to create profits on demand.

Lindberg said: "The new law will create inflation whenever the trusts want inflation...they can unload the stocks on the people at high prices during the excitement and then bring on a panic and buy them back at low prices...the day of reckoning is only a few years removed." That day came with the Stock Market Crash of 1929 and the Great Depression. One of the most critical powers given to the Fed was the right to buy and sell government securities and provide loans to member banks so they can purchase them. This gave a built-in mechanism for profit to the banks whenever government debt was raised. The only thing needed was a way to pay off the debt. This method was created with the income tax in 1913. A national income tax was declared unconstitutional by the Supreme Court in 1895. A constitutional amendment was needed and proposed in Congress - by none other than Senator Nelson Aldrich. It seemed reasonable enough. Income tax on only one percent of income over $20,000, with the promise that it would NEVER increase.

As a graduated tax it would "soak the rich". The rich had other plans. In his 1976 book "The Rockefeller File," Gary Allen said, "by the time the 16th Amendment had been approved by the states, the Rockefeller Foundation was in full operation...about the same time that Judge Kenesaw Landis was ordering the breakup of the Standard Oil monopoly...John D...not only avoided taxes by creating four great tax-exempt foundations; he used them as repositories for his 'divested' interests...made his assets non-taxable so that they might be passed down through generations without...estate and gift taxes...Each year the Rockefellers can dump up to half their incomes into their pet foundations and deduct the donations from their income tax." Exchanging owning things for control of the wealth, foundations are also a means to promote interests that benefit the wealthy. Millions of foundation dollars have been donated to causes like promoting the use of drugs and degrading preventive medicine. Many drugs are made from coal tar derivatives, both oil companies and drug manufacturing concerns - many Rockefeller controlled - are the main beneficiaries.

With the means to loan enormous sums to the government through the Federal Reserve, a method to repay the debt with the income tax, and an escape from taxation for the wealthy through foundations, all that remained was a reason to borrow money. In 1914 World War I began, and after American participation national debt rose from $1 billion to $25 billion.

Woodrow Wilson was elected President in 1913, beating incumbent William Howard Taft, who had vowed to veto any laws to establish a central bank. To divide the Republican vote and elect the relatively unknown Wilson, J.P. Morgan and Co. poured money into the candidacy of Teddy Roosevelt and his Progressive Party. According to an eyewitness, Wilson was brought to Democratic Party headquarters in 1912 by Bernard Baruch, a wealthy banker. He received an indoctrination course from those he met, and in return agreed, if elected: to support the projected Federal Reserve and the income tax and listen to advice in case of war in Europe and on the composition of his cabinet. Wilson's top councilor during his two terms was Colonel Edward M. House[33]. House's biographer, Charles Seymour, called him the "unseen guardian angel of the Federal Reserve Act", helping guide it through

Congress. Another biographer wrote that House believed: "...the Constitution, product of eighteenth-century minds...was thoroughly outdated; that the country would be better off if the Constitution could be scrapped and rewritten..." House wrote a book entitled "Philip Dru: Administrator," published anonymously in 1912. The hero, Philip Dru, rules America and introduces radical changes, such as a graduated income tax, a central bank, and a league of nations!

World War I created a large national debt and huge profits for those who had backed Wilson. Baruch was appointed head of the War Industries Board, exercising dictatorial power over the national economy. He and the Rockefellers were said to have earned over $200 million during the war. Cleveland Dodge, another Wilson backer, sold munitions to the allies, while J.P. Morgan loaned them hundreds of millions, with the protection of U.S. entry into the war. While profit was certainly a motive, the war also was used to justify the notion of world government. William Hoar reveals in his book "Architects of Conspiracy" that the 1950s saw government investigators examining the records of the Carnegie Endowment for International Peace, a long-time globalist organization, found that before World War I, Carnegie trustees planned to involve the U.S. in war to set up world government. The only obstacle was that Americans did not want involvement in European wars. Some kind of inducement - like the explosion of the battleship Main, which provoked the Spanish American war - would have to be staged as provocation. When the Lusitania, carrying 128 Americans on board was sunk by a German submarine, the inducement was met, and anti-German sentiment was aroused. When war was declared, U.S. propaganda painted all Germans as Huns, and all anti-war Americans as traitors. What was not revealed at the time was that the Lusitania was transporting arms and munitions to England, making it a legitimate target for the Germans. Even so, they took out large ads in the New York papers, asking that Americans not to travel on this ship. The evidence points to a deliberate plan to have the ship sunk by the Germans. Colin Simpson, author of "The Lusitania," wrote that "Winston Churchill, head of the British Admiralty during the war, had ordered a report to predict the political impact if a passenger ship carrying Americans was sunk. German naval codes had been broken by the British, who knew approximately where all U-boats near the British Isles were located." According to Simpson, Commander Joseph Kenworthy, of British Naval Intelligence, said: "The Lusitania was deliberately sent at considerably reduced speed into an area where a U-boat was known to be waiting...escorts withdrawn." Wilson had been reelected in 1916 with the slogan "He kept us out of war," but America found itself fighting a European war. Exactly the opposite. Colonel House had negotiated an agreement with England, committing the U.S. to the conflict. The American public had no say in the matter.

With the end of the war and the Versailles Treaty, which called for severe war reparations from Germany, the way was perfectly paved for a leader in Germany like Hitler. Wilson came to the Paris Peace Conference with his "fourteen points," with point fourteen being a "general association of nations," which was to be the first step toward the goal of One World Government. The League of Nations[34].

Wilson's biographer, Ray Stannard Baker, said that the League was not Wilson's idea. "...not a single idea--in the Covenant of the League was original with the President." Colonel House was the author of the Covenant, and Wilson had rewritten it to match to his own wording. The League of Nations was established, but it and the plan for world government eventually failed because the U.S. Senate would not ratify the Versailles Treaty. Pat Robertson, in "The New World Order," states that Colonel House, along with other internationalists, realized that America would not join any scheme for world government without a change in public opinion. After a series of meetings an "Institute of International Affairs", with two branches, in the United States and England was be formed. The British branch became the Royal Institute of International Affairs, with leadership provided by members of the Round Table. (Begun in the late 1800's by Cecil Rhodes, the Round Table aimed to federate the English-speaking peoples of the world and bring it under their rule.)

The Council on Foreign Relations (CFR) was the American branch in New York on July 29, 1921. Founding members included Colonel House, and "...such potentates of international banking as J.P. Morgan, John D. Rockefeller, Paul Warburg, Otto Kahn, and Jacob Schiff...the same clique which had engineered the establishment of the Federal Reserve System," according to Gary Allen in the October 1972 issue of American Opinion. The founding president of the CFR was John W. Davis, J.P. Morgan's personal attorney, while the vice-president was Paul Cravath, also representing the Morgan interests. Professor Carroll Quigley character-ized the CFR as "...a front group for J.P. Morgan and Company in association with the very small American Round Table Group." With time Morgan's influence was lost to the Rockefellers, who found that a one world government fit their philosophy of business well. As John D. Rockefeller, Sr. had said "Competition is a sin", and global monopoly fit their needs as they grew inter-nationally.

Research fellow for the Hoover Institution for War, Revolution, and Peace at Stanford University, Antony Sutton, wrote of this philosophy: "While monopoly control of industries was once the objective of J.P. Mor-gan and J.D. Rockefeller, by the late nineteenth century the inner sanctums of Wall Street understood the most efficient way to gain an unchallenged monopoly was to go political and make society go to work for the monop-olists-- under the name of the public good and the pub-lic interest." Frederick C. Howe revealed the strategy of using government in a 1906 book, "Confessions of a Monopolist": "These are the rules of big business...Get a monopoly; let society work for you; and remember that the best of all business is politics..."

As corporations went global, national monopolies could no longer protect their interests. What was needed was a one world system of government controlled from behind the scenes. This had always been the plan since the time of Colonel House, and to implement it was necessary to weaken the U.S. politically and economically.

The 1920's saw America blessed with a decade of prosperity fueled by the availability of easy credit. From 1923 to 1929 the Fed expanded the money supply by sixty-two percent. The stock market crash of 1929 ruined many small investors but not insiders. In March of 1929 Paul Warburg issued a tip the Crash was coming, and the really large investors exited the market. This according to Allen and Abraham in "None Dare call it Conspiracy." With fortunes intact, these insiders were able to buy companies for a fraction of their worth. Shares that had sold for a dollar might now cost a nickel, and the buying power, and wealth, of the rich increased enormously.

Louis McFadden, Chairman of the House Banking Committee declared: "It was not accidental. It was a carefully contrived occurrence. International bankers sought to bring about a condition of despair here so that they might emerge as rulers of us all[35]." Curtis Dall, son-in-law of FDR and a syndicate manager for Lehman Brothers, an investment firm, was on the N.Y. Stock Exchange floor the day of the crash. In "FDR: My Exploited Father-In-Law," he states: "...it was the calculated 'shearing of the public by the World-Money powers triggered by the planned sudden shortage of call money in the New York Market."

The Crash paved the way for the Wall Street groomed man for the presidency[36], FDR. advertised as a man of the little people, Roosevelt's family had been involved in New York banking since the eighteenth century. They were rich on top of rich. Frederic Delano, FDR's uncle, served on the original Federal Reserve Board. FDR attended Groton and Harvard, and in the 1920's worked on Wall Street, sitting on the board of directors of eleven corporations. Dall wrote of his father-in-law: "...Most of his thoughts, his political ammunition was carefully manufactured for him in advance by the CFR-One World Money group. Brilliantly... he exploded that prepared ammunition in the middle of an unsuspecting target, the American people--and thus paid off and retained his internationalist political support." FDR's removal of America from the gold standard in 1934 opened the way to unrestrained money supply expansion, decades of inflation - and credit revenues for banks. Gold prices rose from $20 an ounce to $35 and gave international bankers large profits.

The New Deal, FDR's most remembered program, was financed through heavy borrowing[37]. Those who had caused the Depression loaned America the money to recover from it. Then, through the National Recovery Administration, proposed by Bernard Baruch in 1930, they were placed in control of regulating the economy. FDR appointed Baruch his disciple Hugh Johnson to run the NRA, working with CFR member Gerard Swope. With broad powers to control wages, prices, and working conditions, it was as Herbert Hoover wrote in his memoirs: "...pure fascism; merely a remaking of Mussolini's corporate state..." The Supreme Court soon ruled the NRA unconstitutional.

During the FDR years, the Council on Foreign Relations captured the political life of the U.S. Besides Treasury Secretary Morgenthau, other CFR members included Secretary of State Edward Stettinus, War Secretary Henry Stimson, and Assistant Secretary of State Sumner Welles. Since 1934 almost every United States Secretary of State has been a CFR member; and ALL Secretaries of War or Defense, from Henry L. Stimson through the present. The CIA has been under CFR control since its creation, starting with Allen Dulles, founding member of the CFR and brother of Secretary of State under President Eisenhower, John Foster Dulles. Allen Dulles had been at the Paris Peace Conference and joined the CFR in 1926 later becoming its president. John Foster Dulles had been a protégés Woodrow Wilson's at the Paris Peace Conference. A founding member of the CFR and an in-law of the Rockefellers, Chairman of the Board of the Rockefeller Foundation, and Board Chairman of the Carnegie Endowment for International Peace.

In 1940 FDR defeated internationalist Wendell Willkie, who wrote a book entitled "One World," and later became a CFR member. Congressman Usher Burdick protested at the time on the floor of the House that Willkie was being financed by J.P. Morgan and New York utility bankers. Polls showed few Republicans favored him, yet the media portrayed him as THE Republican candidate. Since that time nearly ALL presidential candidates have been CFR members. President Truman - not a member - was advised by a group of "wise" CFR members, according to Gary Allen. In 1952 and 1956, CFR member Adlai Stevenson challenged CFR member Eisenhower.

In 1963, John F. Kennedy was probably killed because he had the courage NOT to go along with all their plans. In 1964 the GOP shocked the Establishment by nominating Barry Goldwater over Nelson Rockefeller. Rockefeller and the CFR moved to paint Barry Goldwater as a dangerous radical. In 1968 CFR[38] Nixon ran against CFR Humphrey. The 1972 election featured CFR Nixon vs. CFR McGovern. CFR candidates for president have included George McGovern, Walter Mondale, Edmund Muskie, John Anderson, and Lloyd Bentsen. In 1976 we had Jimmy Carter, who is a member of the Trilateral Commission. Ronald Reagan was not a member of the CFR, but his Vice-President was a member of both the CFR and the Trilateral Commission and CFR director (1977-79) George H.W. Bush - though his name strangely disappears from the membership list in 1979. And last but not least, CFR member Bill Clinton. Both Bush and Kerry are very close to the CFR drawing most of their top foreign and economic policy advisers from this elite organization. The CFR saw that Obama, young and inexperienced, would need to gather around himself members of the Council on Foreign Relations.

Most (excluding Reagan) have all promoted the New

World Order, controlled by the United Nations. The problem is that "...the present United Nations organization is actually the creation of the CFR and is housed on land in Manhattan donated to it by the family of chairman David Rockefeller," as described by Pat Robertson. The original concept for the UN was the outcome of the Informal Agenda Group, formed in 1943 by Secretary of State Cordell Hull. All except Hull were CFR members, and Isaiah Bowman, a founding member of the CFR, originated the idea. The American delegation to the San Francisco meeting that drafted the charter of the United Nations in 1949 included CFR members Nelson Rockefeller, John Foster Dulles, John McCloy, and CFR members who were communist agents - Harry Dexter White, Owen Lattimore, and the Secretary-General of the conference, Alger Hiss. In the CFR sat forty-seven of its members in the United States delegation controlling the outcome.

Since that time the CFR the representatives mass media - mostly controlled by CFR members - like the Washington Post's Katherine Graham and Henry Luce of Time-Life, foundations, and political groups have lobbied consistently to grant the United Nations more authority and power. Bush and the Gulf War were only one of the recent calls for a New World Order. Obama has taken the banner on plans for the new world order.

The Illuminati, the International Bankers, such as the Rothschilds, the Rockefellers, and other elites, have had 200 years to infiltrate the US government in all major leadership roles. They also control our economy and our military. It would seem that the general public can do nothing to stop them however, as of 2014 there were roughly 324.1 million people in the US. If they would work together the insanity of the International Bankers could be stopped.

And now they are planning to terminate 6.5 billion people from planet Earth!

Why does the Illuminati want to do this? The answer is simple. They envision the world as a pyramid with them at the top and approximately a half billion people to serve their needs. These giants of finance have no compassion for human beings. They do not think as normal people think. Their god is Lucifer. Their ultimate goal is power for power's sake and they are building a platform for the Anti-Christ.

CHAPTER 4: THE ILLUMINATI DEPOPULATION AGENDA

"While the global elite construct underground bunkers, eat organic food and hoard seeds in Arctic vaults; the global poor are being slowly starved thanks to high commodity prices and poisoned with genetically modified (GMO) food. Austerity measures aimed largely at the poor are being imposed on all the nations of the world. Weather events grow more deadly and brushfire wars more frequent. An AK-47 can be bought for $49 in the markets of West Africa. The depopulation campaign of the inbred Illuminati bankers is accelerating," said Dean Henderson on July 12, 2011.

In 1957 President Dwight Eisenhower, who warned the country of the looming dangers of a "military-industrial complex[39]", commissioned a panel of scientists to study overpopulation. The scientists published Alternatives I, II and III[40], advocating the release of deadly viruses and continuous warfare as means to decrease world population. The first supposition dovetailed with the pharmaceutical interests of the Rockefellers. According to Nexus magazine, the Rockefellers own one-half of the US pharmaceutical industry, which would reap billions developing medicines to battle the deadly viruses about to be released. Remember the recent outbreaks in the USA of Ebola and measles? In the case of the measles, it is a disease that was thought to be long defeated. Ebola was considered to be quarantined to Africa only, but it was then invited here in the US by the Obama administration.

In 1969 the Senate Church Committee discovered that

the US Defense Department (DOD) had requested a budget of tens of millions of taxpayer dollars for a program to speed development of new viruses which target and destroy the human immune system. DOD officials testified before Congress that they planned to produce a synthetic biological agent, an agent that does not naturally exist and for which no natural immunity could be acquired. Most important is that it might be refractory to the immunological and therapeutic processes upon which we depend to maintain our relative freedom from infectious disease. House Bill 5090 authorized the funds and MK-NAOMI was carried out at Fort Detrick, Maryland. Out of this research came the AIDS virus which was targeted at undesirable elements of the population. The first AIDS viruses were administered through a massive smallpox vaccine campaign in central and southern Africa by the World Health Organization in 1977. A year later ads appeared in major US newspapers soliciting promiscuous gay male volunteers to take part in a Hepatitis B vaccine study. The program targeted male homosexuals[41] age 20-40 in New York City, Los Angeles, Chicago, St. Louis, and San Francisco. It was administered by the US Centers for Disease Control which, the same department that, under its earlier incarnation as the US Public Health Department in Atlanta, oversaw the Tuskegee syphilis experiments on African American males.

San Francisco has been used in numerous CIA experiments[42], due to its high population of left-leaning and gay citizens, which the Illuminati views as undesirables. According to Dr. Eva Snead[43], San Francisco has one of the highest cancer rates in the country. For years Malathion - first developed by the Nazis - was sprayed over the city by helicopters from the CIA's Evergreen Air, whose Arizona base is used, according to author William Cooper, as CIA transshipment point for Columbian cocaine. The mysterious Legionnaire's Disease occurs often in San Francisco and the CIA's MK-ULTRA mind control bad acid program was based there.

The Bilderberg Group was the intellectual force behind the introduction of AIDS. Author Cooper says the Bilderberg Policy Committee gave orders to DOD to introduce the AIDS virus. The Bilderberg Group is close to the Club of Rome, which was founded on a Rockefeller estate near Bellagio, Italy and is backed by the same European Black Nobility who frequent Bilderberger meetings. A 1968 study by the Club of Rome advocated lowering the birth rate and increasing the death rate. Club founder Dr. Aurelio Peccei made a top-secret recommendation to introduce a microbe that would attack the auto-immune system, then develop a vaccine as a prophylactic for the global elite. One month after the 1968 Club of Rome meeting Paul Ehrlich published The Population Bomb. The book hints at a draconian depopulation plan in the works. On page seventeen Ehrlich writes, "The problem could have been avoided by population control...so that a _death rate solution' did not have to occur." A year later MK-NAOMI was born. Peccei himself authored the Club of Rome's much-touted Global 2000 report, which President Jimmy Carter pushed on his BCCI shakedown cruise of Africa. Peccei wrote in the report, "Man is now vested with unprecedented, tremendous responsibilities and thrown into the role of moderator of life on the planet - including his own."

The Bilderbergers were behind the Haig-Kissinger Depopulation Policy, a driving force at the State Department and administered by the National Security Council. Pressure is applied to Third World countries to reduce their populations. Those that do not comply see their US aid withheld or are subject to Pink Plan low-intensity war that targets civilians, especially women of child-bearing age. In Africa famine and brush-fire wars are encouraged. AK-47 rifles can be bought at West African markets for under $50. The same is true in the markets of Peshawar, Pakistan. In 1975, a year after attending a Club of Rome conference on the topic, then Secretary of State Kissinger founded the Office of Population Affairs (OPA).

Latin American OPA case officer Thomas Ferguson spilled the beans on OPA's agenda when he stated, there is a single theme behind all our work; we must reduce population levels. Either they do it our way, through nice clean methods or they will get the kind of mess that we have in El Salvador, or in Iran, or in Beirut...Once population is out of control it requires authoritarian government, even fascism, to reduce it. The professionals aren't interested in reducing population for humanitarian reasons...Civil wars are somewhat drawn-out ways to reduce population. The quickest way to reduce population is through famine like in Africa. We go into a country and say, here is your damn development plan. Throw it out the window. Start looking at your population...if you don't ...then you'll have an El Salvador or an Iran, or worse, a Cambodia. Ferguson said of El Salvador, —To accomplish what the State Department deems adequate population control, the civil war (run by CIA) would have to be greatly expanded. You have to pull all the males into fighting and kill significant numbers of fertile, child-bearing age females. You are killing a small number of males and not enough fertile females to do the job...If the war went on 30-40 years, you might accomplish something. Unfortunately, we don't have too many instances of this to study.

Report from Iron Mountain[44]:
In 1961 Kennedy Administration officials McGeorge Bundy, Robert McNamara and Dean Rusk, all CFR and Bilderberger members, led a study group which looked into the problem of peace. The group met at Iron Mountain, a huge underground corporate nuclear shelter near Hudson, New York, where CFR think tank The Hudson Institute is located. The bunker contains redundant offices in case of nuclear attack for Exxon Mobil, Royal Dutch/Shell, and JP Morgan Chase. A copy of the group discussions, known as Report from Iron Mountain, was leaked by a participant, and published in 1967 by Dial Press. The report's authors saw war as necessary and desirable stating "...war itself is the basic social system, within which other secondary modes of social organization conflict or conspire. (War is)

the principal organizing force...the essential economic stabilizer of modern societies." The group worried that through "ambiguous leadership the ruling administrative class", might lose its ability to —rationalize a desired war‖, leading to the actual disestablishment of military institutions.

The report goes on to say, — the war system cannot responsibly be allowed to disappear until ... we know exactly what we plan to put in its place ... the possibility of war provides the sense of external necessity without which no government can long remain in power ... the basic authority of a modern state over its people resides in its war powers. War has served as the last great safeguard against the elimination of necessary classes.

False "historian" Howard Zinn described this conundrum when he wrote, "American capitalism needed international rivalry - and periodic war – to create an artificial community of interest between rich and poor, supplanting the genuine community of interest among the poor that showed itself in sporadic movements."

The Iron Mountain gang was not the first to discover the virtues of war. In 1909 the trustees of the Andrew Carnegie Foundation for International Peace met to discuss pre-WWI American life. Many of the participants were members of Skull & Bones. They concluded, "There are no known means more efficient than war, assuming the objective is altering the life of an entire people...how do we involve the United States in a war?"

The Report from Iron Mountain goes on to propose

a proper role for those of the lower classes, crediting military institutions with providing —antisocial elements with an acceptable role in the social structure. The younger and more dangerous of these hostile social groupings have been kept under control by the Selective Service System...A possible surrogate for the control of potential enemies of society is the reintroduction, in some form consistent with modern technology and political process, of slavery...The development of a sophisticated form of slavery may be an absolute prerequisite for social control in a world at peace. The Iron Mountain goons, though thrilled by the idea of slavery, listed as other socioeconomic substitutions for war: a comprehensive social welfare program, a giant open-ended space program aimed at unreachable targets, a permanent arms inspection regime, an omnipresent global police and peacekeeping force, massive global environmental pollution which would require a large labor pool to clean up, socially-oriented blood sports and a comprehensive eugenics program.

The Iraqi genocide fulfilled the dreams of the Club of Rome Zero Population Growth maniacs, while also providing a testing ground for two of the war substitutes proposed by the Iron Mountain fascists: an arms inspection regime and UN peacekeepers. Both concepts gained traction in the international community thanks to the Gulf War.

Estimates of Iraqi casualties during the first Gulf War are sobering. Some organizations like Greenpeace put the death toll at near one million people. It was a war in which the media was denied access on a scale never before seen, so casualty figures vary greatly. According to Tony Murphy, a researcher at the International War Crimes Tribunal, the US attack on Iraq killed 125,000 civilians, while destroying 676 schools, 38 hospitals, 8 major hydroelectric dams, 11 power plants, 119 power substations and half the country's telephone lines. The attacks occurred mostly at night when people were most vulnerable. In the months following the war the death rate of Iraqi children under five tripled. Thirty-eight percent of these deaths were caused by diarrhea. Victor Filatov, a Russian journalist reporting for Sovetskaya Rossiya from post-war Baghdad wrote, what further bloodshed do these barbarians of the 21st century need? I thought the Americans had changed since Vietnam...but no, they never change. They remain true to themselves.

According to former US Attorney General Ramsey Clark, the US was found guilty of nineteen war crimes against Iraq before the International War Crimes Tribunal. The US dropped 88,000 tons of bombs on Iraq during the first Gulf War. Many bombs were tipped with armor piercing depleted uranium (DU) warheads, which may account for chronic Iraqi health problems. Dr. Siegwart-Horst Gunther, a German physician who came to Iraq to help its people, became gravely ill when he handled just one cigar-sized fragment from a DU warhead. Dr. Gunther measured the tiny object's radioactivity to be 11 microSv per hour, whereas an acceptable exposure is no more than 300 microSv per year. Three hundred tons of DU ammunition was deployed during the war. Many believe DU is responsible for Gulf War Syndrome, which has killed and permanently injured many US soldiers who fought in the Persian Gulf Theater. Since 2000, nearly 11,000 US Gulf War veterans have died from Gulf War Syndrome, while the Pentagon continues to cover up this travesty.

Iraqi casualties Second Gulf War: 2003-2013[45]

At a minimum, 134,000 civilians have been killed by war's violence since 2003 in Iraq.

Many deaths in Iraq were unreported or unrecorded: So, the toll of violent death due to war may be 250,000 or more people. The IBC noted, "The current death toll could be around twice the numbers recorded by IBC and the various official sources in Iraq." They hasten to add, however that, "We do not think it could possibly be 10 times higher."

However, a study published in the Lancet, gives a range of between 426,000 and 793,000 killed after the invasion through July 2006.

Source Iraqi casualties March 2003 to ... Iraq Family Health Survey 151,000 violent deaths. June 2006 Lancet survey 601,027 violent deaths out of 654,965 excess deaths. June 2006 Opinion Research

Business survey 1,033,000 violent deaths from the conflict. August 2007 Iraqi Health Ministry 87,215 violent deaths per death certificates issued.

Deaths prior to January 2005 unrecorded.

Health Ministry estimates up to 20% more deaths are undocumented. January 2005 to February 2009 Associated Press 110,600 violent deaths.

Health Ministry death certificates plus AP estimate of casualties for 2003–2004. April 2009 Iraq Body Count 105,052 – 114,731 violent civilian deaths. Compiled from commercial news media, NGO, and official reports.

Over 162,000 civilian and combatant deaths January 2012 WikiLeaks. Classified Iraq war logs 109,032 violent deaths including 66,081 civilian deaths.-January 2004 to December 2009.

Satanism & Psychotronic Warfare:

The US tested many top-secret high-tech weapons systems in the Gulf War. When Iraqi ground forces surrendered, many of them were in a state of delirium and lethargy that could have been induced by extremely low-frequency radio waves, which the US used as a weapon as early as the Vietnam war. Yale University and CIA psychiatrist Dr. Jose Delgado[46] studied mind control for the Company during the 1950's as part of the MK-ULTRA program. Delgado determined, "Physical control of many brain functions is a demonstrated fact...it is even possible to create and follow intentions...By electronic stimulation of specific cerebral structures, movements can be induced by radio command...by remote control."

According to a military document written by Colonel Paul Valley and Major Michael Aquino titled From PSYOP to Mindwar: The Psychology of Victory[47], the US Army used an operational weapons system to map the minds of neutral and enemy individuals and then to change them in accordance with US national interests. The technique was used to secure the surrender of 29,276 armed Viet Cong and North Vietnamese Army soldiers in 1967 and 1968. The US Navy was also heavily involved in psychotronic research. Many US soldiers who served near the DMZ that divided North and South Vietnam claimed to see UFOs on a regular basis. The Pentagon Papers revealed that an electronic barrier was placed along the DMZ by the secretive JASON Society.

Major Michael Aquino was an Army psyops specialist in Vietnam, where his unit specialized in drug-inducement, brainwashing, virus injection, brain implants, hypnosis, and use of electromagnetic fields and extremely low-frequency radio waves. After Vietnam, Aquino moved to San Francisco and founded the Temple of Set[48]. Set is the ancient Egyptian name for Lucifer. Aquino was now a senior US Military Intelligence official. He'd been given a Top-Secret security clearance on June 9, 1981. Less than a month later an Army intelligence memo revealed that Aquino's Temple of Set was an off shoot of Anton La Vey's Church of Satan, also headquartered in San Francisco. Two other Set members were Willie Browning and Dennis Mann. Both were Army Intelligence officers. The Temple of Set was obsessed with military matters and political fascism. It was especially preoccupied with the Nazi Order of the Trapezoid. Aquino's —official‖ job was history professor at Golden Gate College. The Temple recruited the same Hells Angels who Billy Mellon Hitchcock had used to dole out his bad CIA acid. Its members frequented prostitutes where they engaged in all manner of sadomasochistic activities. Director of Army Counter-Intelligence Donald Press revealed that Dennis Mann was assigned to the 306 PSYOPS Battalion and that Aquino was assigned to a top-secret program known as Presidio. Presidio was also the name of a spooky US Army base in what is now the Golden Gate National Recreation Area, which Mikhail Gorbachev reportedly frequented as the Soviet Union was falling apart. Was Aquino part of an operation to map the mind of the Soviet Union's last leader and induce him into proposing both glasnost and perestroika, the two free market policies that ultimately led to the Soviet Union's demise? Remember the curious mark which suddenly appeared on Gorbachev's forehead? Was he implanted with some sort of microchip mind-control device to make him think in accordance with US national interests?

Such Orwellian technology is marketed on a regular basis throughout the world. International Healthline Corporation and others sell microchip implants in the US, Russia, and Europe. The Humane Society has adopted a policy of micro-chipping all stray pets. The State of Hawaii requires that all pets be micro-chipped. Six thousand people in Sweden have accepted a microchip in their hand, which they use for all purchases. Trials are also underway in Japan. In July 2002, National Public Radio reported a similar trial beginning in Seattle. Later in 2002, after a rash of suspicious abductions of young girls, BBC reported that a British company plans to implant children with microchips so that their parents can monitor their whereabouts.

Dr. Carl Sanders, a highly acclaimed electronics engineer, revealed that a microchip project he launched to help people with severed spinal cords was taken over by the Bill Colby's Operation Phoenix in a series of meetings organized by Henry Kissinger. Sanders says the optimal spot for a microchip implant is just below the hairline on a person's forehead, since the device can be recharged by changes in body temperatures, which are most pronounced there. Interestingly, this is the location of the pineal gland or Third Eye. The 1986 Emigration Control Act grants the President the power to mandate any kind of ID he deems necessary. Researchers at Southern California have developed a chip which mimics the hippocampus, the part of the brain that deals with memory. Pentagon officials are interested in using it in experiments to create a - super-soldier. Another microchip called Braingate[49] is being implanted in paralyzed people. It allows them to control their environment by simply thinking.

Psychological warfare in Iraq gave way to slow genocide. According to UNICEF, as of late 2001, 1.5 million Iraqi children had died as a result of sanctions[50], while one child in ten died before their first birthday. Thalassemia, anemia, and diarrhea were the biggest killers and could have been prevented if it not for a chronic shortage of blood and medicine in Iraq due to the sanctions. UN Committee 661 served as arbiter of what constituted a - dual use item and therefore banned for import into Iraq. By 2001, over 1,600 Iraqi contracts with Western companies for medical equipment had been blocked by 661.

The Gulf War decimated Iraq's sewer and water treatment systems. Iraqis were forced to drink polluted water, leading to numerous health problems. Iraq was not allowed to import chlorine to clean the water since 661 deemed it a potential chemical weapon. Electrical power was rationed in three-hour daily increments per household since the Iraqi government couldn't get the parts it needed to fix its power plants after the US bombed its entire power grid. With the devaluation of the Iraqi dinar and the ban on the export of 2.4 million barrels of oil per day, the average Iraqi lived on $2.50 a month- enough to buy a pair of shoes. The only Iraqis not affected were the wealthy elite, who had long ago stashed their savings overseas in US dollars.

UNICEF estimates that 30% of Iraqi children no longer went to school whereas, before the war almost all children attended. Often families could only afford to send one child to school because of the cost of simple things like backpacks, shoes, and notebooks. Rafah Salam

Aziz, Director of Mansour Children's Hospital, said parents were often forced to make the same kinds of decisions about their children's lives. Aziz said, "Many times it's easier for a family to let a baby die rather than let the whole family go hungry and get sick."

In 1996 Clinton Defense Secretary William Perry announced a new military buildup in the Persian Gulf. Soon cruise missiles were again raining down on Baghdad. Many nations now grew weary of both US bombing and the sanctions regime, which was brutalizing the Iraqi people while strengthening the grip of Saddam Hussein. Russian President Boris Yeltsin, whose country signed a deal with Iraq to rebuild its shattered oil sector, said he was disturbed at the use of extreme and radical force against the Arab world. The Russian opposition offered a more scalding appraisal. Alexander Lebed stating angrily, the US is like a strong master who spits on everybody. Turkey, Jordan, and Syria all expressed unease over the new round of bombing. Even the Saudis, where Islamic fundamentalism was on the rise and two major bombings had occurred at US bases, now refused to allow the US to use its bases to bomb Iraq. Many countries, including France, began openly flaunting the UN embargo against Iraq in the late 1990's. Former Assistant Secretary of the UN, Dennis Halliday, who initially headed the UN Humanitarian Program to Iraq, resigned his post in protest. He said sanctions were demolishing the very class of Iraqi people who wanted to create a better government in the country. He was scornful of the UN Oil for Food Program under which the US received 70% of Iraqi oil.

Halliday stated plainly, - We are guilty of committing genocide, through the Security Council, against Iraq.

Halliday's 1998 successor was Hans Van Sponeck, who watched as the UN unfurled the UNSCOM arms inspection regime, paid for by Iraqi oil sales. US inspector Scott Ritter confirmed Iraqi suspicions that UNSCOM was gathering intelligence for CIA and Mossad. UNSCOM was just the latest CIA tool. In 1996 the Iraqi government claimed international relief agencies, including the World Food Program, which claimed to be helping the Kurds, were actually CIA operatives attempting to destabilize the country. In fact, the CIA had spent more than $20 million in its support of the Iraqi National Congress, led by long-time CIA surrogate Jalal Talibani's PKK Kurdish faction. In January 1997 Iraq uncovered two Mossad spy rings in one month following the attempted assassination of Saddam Hussein's son. Hans Van Sponeck had seen enough. He too resigned in protest. In early 1999 it was revealed that the US had used UNSCOM to plant electronic bugging devices in the Iraqi Ministry of Defense. Arms inspector Scott Ritter said the CIA was using UNSCOM to provoke a crisis. In December 1998 UNSCOM, faced with the embarrassing accusations of espionage, pulled out of Iraq. On December 15th, the US launched a new round of bombing. Ritter says intelligence gathered by UNSCOM was used for targeting. UNSCOM spokesman David Kay resurfaced in 2003 calling for a US invasion of Iraq. He now worked for SAIC, which landed numerous Pentagon contracts to rebuild Iraq.

CHAPTER 5: GOVERNMENT CREATED DISEASES

Joyce Riley[51] (R.N.), a Gulf War veteran, and Peter Kawaja, a security systems business owner, have been revealing what they know about the Gulf War illness[52] on radio talk shows. The information they have uncovered regarding the intentional use of germ warfare against U.S. soldiers has shocked many Americans.

According to Joyce Riley, 200,000 Americans are now sick and 7000 have already died from these illnesses. The Veteran's Administration is trying to cover up the "Problem," but still admits that their figures show 5200-6400 have died. The VA admits to giving medical care to 489,400 Gulf War vets in a fax dated 8/18/95. Over 55% became sick from the Gulf War.

Chemicals used in the Gulf War were transported there by the United States. The Desert Storm troops were inoculated and sprayed with these bacteria, which are communicable to family and pets. Millions in the world are sick with this disease; 300,000 have died worldwide.

Drs. Garth and Nancy Nicholson are researching the illness themselves, at their own expense. They have discovered that this germ warfare was tested on death row prison inmates in Huntsville, Alabama. Dr. Nicholson and other doctors working on cures have been threatened with loss of licenses or funding for research.

They have the evidence that all of these viruses were man-made, and treatment is available, but is being withheld by the VA and government officials. Government agents, and even the publisher of Reader's Digest knew that Desert Storm vets came back with EBOLA II which is the carrier form of the illness rather than the terminal form. These carriers are infecting others. Children born to GW vets after the war are dying of various forms of cancer more frequently than in non-Gulf children.

On 2/9/94 the U.S. Senate Committee on Banking, Housing & Urban Affairs issued a press released titled: "Riegle uncovers U.S. shipments of biological warfare related material to Iraq prior to the Gulf war: Wants investigation of link to Gulf War Syndrome[53]."

Schwarzkopf was given authority to use the nerve agent GF. Some people have died just because of handling shipments of this agent to Desert Storm. There are sworn affidavits and all of it ties in with Iran-Contra.

Peter's business, the International Security Group, was

awarded a $1 million security contract for a Product Ingredient Technology (PIT) computer system. PIT was a closed project (contracted for the government) at Boca Raton, Florida.

He found out that the U.S. government was manufacturing germ warfare at PIT. The main U.S. financiers were Bush, Baker, and Jim Duetch. The architect and financier of the project was Dr. Ishan Barboodie, builder of the Pharma-150 chemical/biological complex at Rabta, Libya.

Kawaja uncovered evidence that IBI (Ishan Barbouti International) was working with the feds and PIT. He was told to install a Hydrogen Cyanide detection system for PIT. (A strain of Hydrogen Cyanide called "Prussian Blue" was being tested on gas masks filters for mass penetration). President Bush, Brent Scowcroft (NSC), and U.S. intelligence were behind the testing/use of Prussian Blue, at least two years in advance of the Gulf War, which was planned for this purpose.

He took his concerns about PIT to the CIA, FBI, and U.S. Customs. They had him operate as an undercover agent for them and told him that IBI were international terrorists, and the government was going to prosecute them. However, while collecting intelligence, he found that the U.S. government was working with these "terrorists."

The March 28, 1990, issue of The Tampa Tribune reported that "two U.S. chemical companies have refused to sell the army an ingredient to make poison gas[54]."

Peter told this story on an ABC "Nightline" interview, after which his wife was murdered. Peter was sent a warning from the Pentagon from a Dave McMichaels, that documents had already been made up against Peter and credible people would testify against him. Mr. McMichaels became the victim of multiple stab wounds and is likely dead. Like Whitewater, there are dead bodies everywhere. Every one of Peter's employees are missing: Feared dead. He has a suit against federal agents for treason and war crimes. The government says they're immune because of "national security.[55]"

A War Powers Act search warrant (ordered by George Bush) was issued for Peter's company, after he had sent documents to the National Security Agency on July 12, 1990 and issued warnings of Iraqi intelligence operating in the U.S. Peter asked two questions: 1). Is our military in joint venture with IBI to develop chemical and biological weapons? and 2). Does the President know? The answers to both questions was "yes." As a result, 8 men with automatic weapons paid a visit to Peter, sequestered him under armed guard for 4 hours and removed all evidence, sealing it under the War Powers Act. They told Peter to "shut up" because he knows who manufactured, shipped, and used biological weapons on Desert Storm troops.

Joyce Riley worked as a nurse transporting sick and

injured troops from the Gulf War to the U.S. She stated that 500,000 sick vets have been turned aside from the VA. They were sprayed, inoculated, or given nerve-agent pre-treatment pills that caused their sicknesses. Some who did not take the pills (faked it) have not become ill with the same sickness as fellow soldiers who swallowed the pills.

Men from Desert Storm are bleeding from all parts of the body, seriously ill or dead, and the VA says it's all in their heads. The illnesses are all immune system attackers, and the end result is death from cancers. AIDS and EBOLA viruses are man-made, and EBOLA is coming home with these guys. Peter has the proof. Ft. Detrick is believed to be the place where most likely all antibodies (i.e., cures) to AIDS, EBOLA, and Desert Storm Syndrome, are stored.

This is an outbreak and is catching to anyone, including animals. Nurses who cared for sick vets are now sick and dying as well as their children and pets. Airline passengers have become sick because of riding with ill vets. An overseas airliner has confirmed this. Joyce is very worried because this could be a holocaust for the whole world, not just the United States.

Joyce has started a registry of Gulf War vets[56]. Her phone is (713) 587-5437. If the voice mail is full, please call back. Peter and Joyce state that the government knew two years before Desert Storm that they were going to use germ warfare against the troops, at which time the Joint Chiefs of Staff were shot up with anti-botulism. Eventually they were so immune as to be able to take enough botulism to kill 1000 horses. 100 horses were pastured at Ft. Detrick to get the anti-botulism serum for the Joint Chiefs of Staff. Riley and Kawaja spoke at Kansas City, Missouri, on 8/29/95 regarding the Gulf War Syndrome. During the three days in Kansas City, they were under constant surveillance and Joyce developed a laser burn on her head. Prior to this meeting, on 8/5/95 fumes disrupted a symposium on the Gulf War Syndrome in a Washington, D.C. hotel.

Finally, the VA information on the Gulf War Syndrome, as well as all the evidence that was collected, was stored at the Murrah Federal Building[57] in Oklahoma City, and was reported to have been destroyed in the April 19th explosion that took 168 lives!

The AIDS Virus was planted in Vaccine at the U.N. World Health Organization to weaken and destroy the blacks in the U.S. and around the world. Most Americans know by now that there is no known cure for AIDS. Some of our medical men frankly state that there will never be a cure, except by isolation. They have found that the AIDS virus is so small - It can pass through a condom. And so strong - it can live six hours on a kitchen table!

But the most amazing news is that doctors have discovered that the AIDS' virus was prepared especially for the African Black Man by Communist agents working as scientists for the World Health Organization. [They are trough with the Blacks, as they have served their purpose in destroying Civil Rights and other laws they did not like in America. The Blacks never suspecting their role as they worked tirelessly for equality, they never, and still do not, realize; that instead of getting what they most wanted, the Blacks were instead losing ground until, today their condition in life has not become better; But has steadily grown worse. Therefore, the so-called Black leaders like Jessie Jackson and the Rev. Sharp will lead them to total destruction like a Judas Goat, for it is now time to remove them because they are becoming increasingly harder to handle]. They decided that our conquest by AIDS would be easier and more effective than a nuclear holocaust.

Dr. William Campbell Douglass, an M.D. wrote an article for the September issue of "Health Freedom News," the journal of the National Health Federation entitled: Who Murdered Africa? This is not a question. It's a statement. The World Health Organization (WHO) murdered Africa with the AIDS virus. Dr. Douglass continues: Other suspects, the homosexuals, the green monkey, and the Haiti and, were only pawns in this Viricidal Attack on the non-Communist World. Many viruses grow in animals and many grow in humans, but most of the viruses that affect animals don't affect humans. There are exceptions, such as Yellow Fever and Smallpox.

The World Health Organization, in published articles,

called for scientists to work with these deadly agents and attempt to make a Hybrid Virus that would be deadly to the Black Man. (Allison, Bulletin, WHO 1972, 47:257-63) In the bulletin of the World Health Organization (WHO), Volume 47, pp. 251, 1972, they said, "An attempt should be made to see if Viruses can in fact exert selective effects on immune function. The possibility should be looked into that the immune response to the virus itself may be impaired if the infecting Virus damages, more or less selectively, the cell responding to the Virus."

That's AIDS. What the WHO is saying in plain English is, "Let's cook up a virus that selectively destroys the T-cell system of man, an Acquired Immune Deficiency."

Why would anyone wish to do this? If you destroy the T-cell System of man, you destroy man. Is it even remotely possible that the World Health Organization would want to develop a virus that would wipe out the Black Race? If their new virus creation worked, the WHO stated, then many terrible and fatal infectious viruses could be made even more terrible and more malignant. Does this strike you as being a peculiar goal for a HEALTH organization?

What about the green monkey? Some of the best virologists in the world and many of those directly involved in AIDS research, such as Robert Gallo and Luc Montagnier, have said that the green monkey may be the culprit. You know the story: A green monkey bit a native on the rump and, bam -- AIDS all over Central Africa. There is a fatal flaw here. Gallo, Montagnier and these other virologists know that the AIDS virus doesn't occur naturally in monkeys.

In fact, it does not occur naturally in any animal! AIDS started practically simultaneously in the United States, Haiti, Brazil, and Central Africa. One would wonder - was the green monkey a jet pilot? Examination of the gene structure of the green monkey cells proves that it is not genetically possible to transfer AIDS virus from monkeys to man by natural means.

Dr. Theodore Strecker's research indicates that the National Cancer Institute in collaboration with the World Health Organization made the AIDS virus in their laboratories at Ft. Detrick (now NCI). They combined the deadly retroviruses, bovine leukemia virus and sheep visna virus, and injected them into human tissue cultures. The result was the AIDS virus, the first human retrovirus known to man and now believed to be 100% fatal to those infected. The momentous plague that the world now faces was anticipated by the National Academy of Sciences (NAS) in 1974 when they recommended that "Scientists throughout the world join with the members of this committee in voluntarily deferring experiments (linking) animal viruses."

What the NAS is saying in carefully guarded English is: "For God's sake, stop this madness!"

Now that we've let the green monkey off the hook, how about the Communists (read that International Zionist)? Well, the Communists are saying AIDS is a "capitalist plot."

This should make you suspicious because, as any student of the Zionist conspiracy knows, they (the Jews) always blame others for what they are in the process of doing. And what they are doing is Conducting Germ Warfare from Fort Detrick, Maryland, and Tel Aviv, Israel against the free world, especially the United States, even using foreign Communist agents within the United States Army's germ warfare unit euphemistically called the Army Infectious Disease Unit.

Carlton Gajdusek, a NIH executive at Fort Detrick, admits it: "In the facility I have a building where more Communist Scientists from the U.S.S.R. and Mainland China work (with full passkeys to all the laboratories) than there are Americans. Even the Army's Infectious Disease Unit is loaded with foreign workers, not always friendly nationals."

Can you imagine that? A United Nations - WHO Communist Trojan horse in our biological warfare center. There is absolutely no doubt that the creations of the AIDS virus by the WHO was not just a scientific exercise that got out of hand.

It was a cold-blooded, diabolical, successful attempt to

create a killer virus that was then used in a successful experiment in Africa. So successful that most of Central Africa may be wiped out, 75,000,000 dead within the next few years.

It was not an accident. It was deliberate. In the Federation Proceedings of the United States in 1972, WHO said: "In the relation to the immune response a number of useful experimental approaches can be visualized."

They suggested that a neat way to do this would be to put their new killer virus (AIDS) into a vaccination program, sit back and observe the results. "This would be particularly informative in Subships," they said. That is, Give the AIDS virus to brothers and sisters and see if they die, who dies first and of what, just like using rats in a laboratory. They used Smallpox and Hepatitis Vaccine for their vehicle and the geographical sites chosen in 1972 were Uganda and other African states, Haiti, Brazil, and Japan.

Dr. Strecker pointed out that even if the African green monkey could transmit AIDS to humans, the present known amount of infection in Africa makes it statistically impossible for a single episode, such as a monkey biting someone on the butt, to have brought this epidemic to the point it currently is. The doubling time of the number of people infected, about every 14 months, when correlated with the first known case, and the present known number of cases, prove beyond a doubt that a large number of people had to have been infected at the same time. From 1972 to 1987 is 15 years. In 15 years, from a single source of infection there would be about 8,000 cases in Africa, not 75 million.

We are approaching World War II mortality statistics. Dr. Theodore A. Strecker is the courageous doctor who unraveled this conundrum, The Greatest Murder Mystery (A mystery to most Americans, who have been deceived into believing there is no conspiracy to destroy Christianity and Christians from off the face of the earth)of all Time. He should get the Nobel Prize, but he'll be lucky not to be "suicided with a heart attack or accident of some sort."

Strecker has found that The AIDS epidemic will in all probability bankrupt the nation's medical system. He became fascinated with the peculiar scientific anomalies concerning AIDS that kept cropping up. Why did "experts" keep talking about green monkeys and homosexuals being the culprits when it was obvious that the AIDS virus was a man-made virus? Why did they say that it was a homosexual and drug user disease when in Africa it was obviously a heterosexual disease?

If the green monkey did it, then why did AIDS explode practically simultaneously in Africa, Haiti, Brazil, the United States and Southern Japan? It performed in this way: because it was deliberately planted, to destroy a people who has become too dangerous to be allowed to live.

As early as 1970 the World Health Organization was growing deadly sheep and bovine viruses in human tissue cultures. Cedric Mims said in a published article in 1981 that there was a Bovine Virus Contaminating the Culture Media of the WHO. Was this an accident? If it was an accident, why did WHO continue to use the vaccine?

This viral and genetic death bomb, AIDS, was finally produced in 1974. It was given to monkeys, and they died of Pneumocystis carinii pneumonia, which is typical of AIDS. Dr. R.J. Biggar said in Lancet: "...The AIDS agent...could not have originated de Novo." That means it didn't come out of thin air. AIDS was engineered in a laboratory by Virologists.

There are 9,000 to the Fourth Power possible AIDS viruses. There are 9,000 base pairs on the genome. So, the fun has just begun. Some will cause brain rot similar to the sheep virus, some leukemia-like diseases from the cow virus, and some that won't do anything. So, the virus will be constantly changing and trying out new esoteric diseases on hapless man. We're only at the beginning.

Because of the trillions of possible genetic combinations, there will never be a vaccine. If they could develop a vaccine, they would undoubtedly give us something equally bad as they did with the polio vaccine - cancer of the brain, the swine flu vaccine - a polio-like disease, the smallpox vaccine (AIDS), and the hepatitis vaccine (AIDS).

This is not the first time the virologists have brought us disaster. SV-40 from monkey cell cultures contaminated polio cultures. Most people in their 40's are now carrying this virus through contaminated polio inoculations given in the early 60s. It is known to cause brain cancer, which explains the increase in this disease that has been observed in the past ten years.

This is the origin of the green monkey theory. The polio vaccine was grown on green monkey kidney cells. Despite the fact that Polio was rapidly disappearing without any medical intervention, 64-million Americans were vaccinated with SV-40 contaminated vaccine in the 60s, producing an increase in cancer of the brain. Primary multifocal leukoencephalopathy (PML), brain rot, has been added to the burden of homosexuals who have been given AIDS through Hepatitis-B Vaccine.

The AIDS virus didn't exist in the United States before 1978. What happened in 1978 to cause AIDS to burst upon the scene and devastate the homosexual and Black segments of our population? It was the introduction of the Hepatitis-B Vaccine which exhibits the exact Epidemiology of AIDS.

A Jewish Doctor W. Schmugner, born in Poland and educated in Russia, came to this country in 1969. By an unexplained process, he became head of the New York City Blood Bank. How does a Jewish Russian-trained doctor become head of one of the largest blood banks in the world? Doesn't that strike you as peculiar? He set up the rules for the hepatitis vaccine studies. Only males between the ages of 20 and 40, who were not monogamous, would be allowed to participate in this study. Can you think of any reason, other than the desire to spread something among the population, for insisting that all those subjected to these experiments be promiscuous? Schmugner is now dead, and his diabolical secret went with him.

The hepatitis vaccine, unlike the AIDS vaccine, was not grown from human tissue culture, so accidental contamination didn't occur. The AIDS Virus was put in the vaccine deliberately. It was no mistake. It affects, almost exclusively, gays, Negroes, Jews, and mixed breeds. The Centers for Disease Control reported in 1981 that four percent of those receiving the hepatitis-vaccine were AIDS-infected. In 1984 they admitted to 60%. Now they refuse to give out figures at all because they don't want to admit that 100% of Hepatitis Vaccine receivers are infected with AIDS. Where is the data on the hepatitis vaccine studies? FDA? CDC? No, The Federal Government has it buried where you will never see it. (Taken in part from The Fact Finder - Phoenix, Ariz.)

CHAPTER 6: SWINE FLU CREATED IN LAB AS A BIOWEAPON?

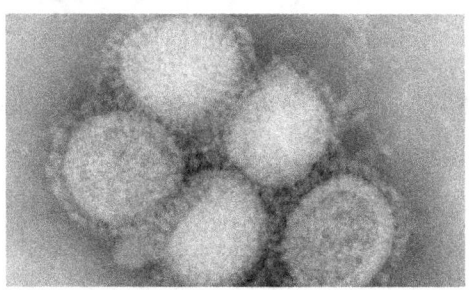

Swine Flu[58], Ebola and HIV were produced in laboratories. The report from Mexico City claims that one of the leading UN scientists discovered certain joint transmission vectors, that is, the transmission of the swine flu virus is similar to the transmission of the Ebola virus and of the HIV/AIDS virus, which indicates that they were genetically modified with the aim of being military bioweapons.

The UN scientist is convinced that the swine flu virus, A-H1N1, and Ebola and HIV viruses were in fact manufactured biological weapons.

As proof, they state that the usual process of transmission is that the virus is transmitted from a pig to a human, which is not the case in this outbreak because no case of a pig being infected with the A-H1N1 virus has been registered. Furthermore, the A-H1N1 virus partly contains American pig genes, partly human and bird flu strains and the virus of the Euro-Asian swine flu.

American military responsible: The other reporter, from Jakarta, claims that World Health Organization leaders are worried that the current swine flu virus has been genetically modified to be transmitted from one species to another because of the fact that the A-H1N1 virus contains the genetic material of the H5N1 virus, that is, bird flu.

Allegedly, American scientists exhumed the body of a woman who died of the Spanish flu in 1918 and used the genetic material of the flu virus as the basis for the creation of the H5N1 virus through genetic ma-nipulation. All this happened in laboratories at the Fort Detrick military base from which the new strain of an-thrax called Ames originated.

We have been taken to the cleaners many times -- The Great Depression -- Threat of communism -- war after war -- Savings and Loan Crisis $500 billion -- Oil em-bargo -- our new financial crisis – Trillions.

War in Iraq -- second largest oil field -- we use 25% of the world's oil -- we truck food and goods on average 1500 miles -- we drive alone is our vehicles -- we just don't want to look too deep !

The U.S. taxpayer is getting raped by a government controlled by the Illuminati!

I know of only two men in Congress worthy of being
called Congressmen – Dr. Ron Paul and Dennis Kucinich.[59]

Ron Paul, Dennis Kucinich won't soon be forgotten In
2007, Dennis Kucinich, a Democrat, and Ron Paul, a
Republican, were kindred spirits: Demure in size, but
mighty in spirit, the congressmen were steadfast in
their outsized battle to change American foreign policy
as they sought the presidency.

"As the Democratic [presidential] nominee I'd consider Ron Paul as my running mate," Kucinich said without hesitation during a 2007 interview with Free Minds TV. He and I agree tremendously on international policy. You might see a vote being 235 to 2 in Congress; you'll know who the two are: Kucinich and Paul. Though successful in forging a friendly and admirable bipartisan bridge on issues of war and largely peace, neither was successful in their 2008 presidential bids. And now both men, who prided themselves on political integrity and purity, grass-roots base and a lack of corporate and lobbyist affiliations have been moved off the political stage, perhaps for good. Brimming with political will and spirit, but short on money, the two doves have flown into the proverbial political coop. On Monday, Paul effectively ended his campaign, after he said he would stop spending money in the 11 states with upcoming party primaries. Previously, he had announced that he will be retiring from the House of Representatives.

In March, Kucinich, of Toledo, lost his congressional seat to Rep. Marcy Kaptur, also a progressive Democrat from Toledo, and one of the longest-serving women in the House. It just seemed like yesterday Kucinich was not far from Paul's mind, when Paul mirthfully stated during a ReLOVEution presidential campaign interview that if elected he'd consider putting the liberal Ohio congressman in his administration, creating a Department of Peace, where the peace-loving Kucinich could really shine. "You've got to give credit to people who think", Paul said of Kucinich at a breakfast sponsored by the Christian Science Monitor, as reported by the Hill on Sept. 21, 2011.

Like the photographic inversion of monochromatic mirror images, Kucinich and Paul reflected each other in their general antiwar stance, foreign policy views and civil-liberty reservations about what they and their supporters perceive as our modern-day surveillance state. While political outliers in their respective parties, they both asked tough questions that challenged us morally and encouraged reflection.

Kucinich recently gave a commencement speech at the American University of Dubai in the United Arab Emirates emphasizing the significance of world peace and harmony given our global interdependence. Kucinich, who often questioned whether our policy of preemptive war had evolved into permanent warfare, suggested to the graduating class that each nation should create a cabinet of peace to help cultivate a sustainable ecosystem of global peace and accord. Ron Paul, a noninterventionist by nature, opposed what he called the terrible cost of war. A staunch civil libertarian, Paul evoked the admonition of Benjamin Franklin, "Those who would give up essential liberty, to purchase a little temporary safety, deserve neither liberty nor safety", when arguing against expansion of war and domestic surveillance to enhance national security.

In attempts to atone for racist newsletter allegations,

Paul would go on to state the obvious and attack the war on drugs as racist and discriminatory. He also highlighted the fact that he provided medical services to black and interracial couples as an ob/gyn doctor at a time when many other white members of his profession would not.

In the bellicose Shakespearean wilderness of pride, pomp and circumstance of glorious war, this world has become, perhaps it's time for that bipartisan cabinet of peace that Kucinich called for during his recent commencement address, to develop social structures for peace and strategies to avert conflict between groups and between states. What a fitting memorial to two departed advocates of global peace and understanding. They may be gone from politics, but they won't soon be forgotten. Their political legacies no doubt will live on -- how is yet to be seen.

But neither of these great men of peace can stand against the evil forces that rule governments and economies, that own most of the world's wealth, that create wars to depopulate the planet, that create diseases to kill off millions, and pull the strings of puppet leaders who have sold their souls for prestige and temporal power. It is a sad thing to know that we are getting raped and cannot do a damn thing about it.

This book is my eighth published work. A neighbor who has read all of my books stopped by with a question:

"You write about the Illuminati who control most of the world's governments and economies. Are you not afraid that they will send black helicopters to kill you for writing against them?"

I remembered Dr. Ron Paul's statement and so I paraphrased it for my neighbor friend.

"If fear keeps me from writing truth, I don't deserve freedom, security, or even life itself."

She didn't speak for several minutes and then said:

"I read your first book "Unto These Hills." It spoke about your people, about the Cherokee Holocaust, when the Cherokee were driven from their homes in the Cherokee Mountains of Western North Carolina and marched   in the dead of winter to Oklahoma Territory in 1838-39. In that book you stated that more than fifteen thousand Cherokee made that march and that almost five thousand died along the way. Is that why you are so outspoken?"

"No, that is not the reason, I replied. I am not alone in speaking out. In England there is David Icke. In Austin, Texas, there is Alex Jones, and there is Jim Marrs and Bill Cooper who are very outspoken.

I have a few more papers left to send to my readers and my "farewell" paper, but this needed to get sent out immediately. In a nutshell: two weeks ago, on a nighttime broadcast simulcast through a number of national radio stations, William Cooper, ex-Naval Intelligence officer, blew his Top-Secret security clearance by putting together a press conference where he laid out the structure of this country's SHADOW GOVERN-MENT, tracing its roots to the UFO/Alien cover-ups that began in the 1940s-1950s.

He was very concise and explicit, naming names, providing documentation, offices, and meetings from the 50s on up to the1970s. He literally ripped the lid off the cover-up and told his audience that he'd probably be killed for this. He was. This brilliant, decorated military career man left Naval Intelligence in 1975. By his own admission, he was unable to reconcile what he'd learned while in Naval Intelligence, about Alien controls and secret combinations within our government. He refused to serve the anti-constitutional "Military Industrial Complex" run by NAS/CIA and the NWO and resigned.

After this he began to leak information, often receiving threats on his life and family for so doing. He continued undaunted but has been increasingly harassed for his outspoken whistleblowing. Two weeks ago, he decided he could no longer hold back what he'd learned, and blew the whistle on the whole charade, naming people's names, dates places...everything he'd learned! Apparently this was the last straw? William Cooper's stunning presentation was bound to get him killed. He knew it and stated it before his live audience. If anyone thinks this man's statements were exaggerated, ask yourself WHY he was killed? There is tight security surrounding the details of the actual incident resulting in his death.

The story is being spun to make it sound like he had a scuffle with two Sheriff deputies in which he shot one officer in the head twice. He was then, according to the official story, shot dead. The deputy is said to be alive, but Cooper was killed on the spot. You can bet your three-dollar bills and wooden nickels that the truth surrounding this little "assassination" will never be revealed before it is spun beyond recognition. There is little doubt that Bill simply went too far. This is the same sort of thing that got Kennedy shot. If "they" kill presidents to cover up these truths, how much chance does one lone ex-military officer have? My own research corroborates every aspect of what Bill had to say in those areas where his subset of information intersects my own. His expertise and knowledge, however, was of a military/political nature (governmental, historical and cover-ups) nature, not specifically scientific.

Yet what he had to say rings true as far as the technological aspects of UFO technology is concerned, as well as some of the truths he mentioned concerned with the nature and motive operandi of the "Gray" aliens, as I have come to understand them.

This is tragic news but before he died, he awakened many people from their sleep. And now there is a new crop of writers and speakers who are not afraid to speak and write their minds.

For information on ordering the incredible 2-hour William Cooper press conference on tape, call the KTTK Radio station at: (801) 759-1581. They broadcast live from 6 to 7 am, Monday thru Friday; and on Saturday and Sunday at 7 to 9 pm, as "k-talk" Radio am 630 ---- in the Provo Utah area. The night of the broadcast their broadcast was interrupted by what was likely a triangle ship EM pulse weapon. Since then, several other broadcasts have been so targeted, and disruptions have occurred as Federal officials have begun harassing the station and interrupting broadcasts by demanding access to studio files during peak broadcast periods. This harassment has been going on quietly across the nation, the target being "talk radio stations NOT with the "plan." This does not include all of what one might think of as "right wing" talk shows. Shows like Rush Limbaugh's and CIA disinformation agent provocateurs like Art Bell, are sure to continue unabated.

In this researcher's opinion there are few great stations left, among these I rank KTTK radio, and the Jeff Rense "Sightings" show among the best. Especially good (less the Gaia oriented new-aged philosophical rhetoric) is the Laura Lee show. I do not agree 100% with any of these shows, but they all present interesting non-main-stream scientific information and all three people running these outfits appear genuinely interested in the truth.

Our deepest sympathies go out to the family of William Cooper. He died a true patriot and with a clear conscience.

May we all be as faithful to our principles as this man. This is yet another WAKE-UP CALL to anyone who doubts that we have entered a NEW era. Bill deliberately got this meeting aired before the Senate and House passed their fascist new "Patriot/USA" act-bills.

Bill Cooper is dead now. Many of us feel that Cooper was killed because of his views.

We know about the evil that exists and the people behind it. And so, we write about it, speak about it. The Illuminati and the many secret societies they work through is a quagmire of spider webs. It takes a lot of research to unravel the web and understand it. Most people don't have the time to devote to the research required. Most of their time is spent in raising families, sports, television, and such. But there are a few people who think for themselves, who read our books and listen to our speeches. These will be the next crop of writers and speakers. David Icke, of England, made a statement that I subscribe to. Revolution and violence will not defeat the Illuminati and their minions. This is not the way. Non-compliance is the answer. If the world's people stand in one voice and say we do not buy your bullshit, and we will not comply with your edicts no matter what. The only avenue left to the Illuminati is to kill everyone on planet earth, which they intend to do anyway. A journey from here to there starts with one step.

"I do not understand what drives you, she said."

"It is my love for life and people", I replied. "The Luciferian Illuminati 13 bloodline families do not understand that. Pull that up on your computer and educate yourself." My friend left shaking her head.

The New World Order has arrived. It's time to be afraid...VERY afraid.

PDD 51 & New Executive Order Give

Obama Dictator Power. An Obama executive order that creates a council of state governors who will work with the feds to expand military involvement in domestic security, together with PDD 51, a Bush era executive order that gives the President dictatorial power in times of national emergency, eliminate the last roadblocks to declaring martial law in the United States.

The new order, which is entitled Establishment of the Council of Governors (PDF), creates a body of ten state governors directly appointed by Obama who will work with the federal government to help advance the synchronization and integration of State and Federal military activities in the United States. The governors will liaise with officials from Northcom, Homeland Security, the National Guard as well as DOD officials from the Pentagon in order to strengthen further the partnership between the Federal Government and State governments, according to the executive order.

The executive order combines seamlessly with Presidential Decision Directive 51 to hand Obama dictator status in times of declared, and not necessarily genuine, national emergency.

In May 2007, former President George W. Bush sparked much alarm by openly declaring himself to be a dictator in the event of a national emergency under provisions that effectively nullify the U.S. constitution, but such an infrastructure has been in place for over 70 years, and this merely represented a re-authorization of martial law powers.

Legislation signed on May 9, 2007, declares that in the event of a catastrophic event?, the President can take total control over the government and the country, bypassing all other levels of government at the state, federal, local, territorial, and tribal levels, and thus ensuring total unprecedented dictatorial power.

The National Security and Homeland Security Presidential Directive, which also places the Secretary of Homeland Security in charge of domestic security?, was signed earlier without the approval or oversight of Congress and seemingly supersedes the National Emergency Act which allows the president to declare a national emergency but also requires that Congress have the authority to modify, rescind, or render dormant? such emergency authority if it believes the president has acted inappropriately. Journalist Jerome Corsi, who studied the directive, also states that it makes no reference to Congress and its language appears to negate any requirement that the president submit to Congress a determination that a national emergency exists.

In July 2007, Congressman Peter DeFazio (D – OR) was asked by his constituents to see what was contained within the classified portion of the White House plan for operating the government after a terrorist attack. Since DeFazio also sits on the Homeland Security Committee and has clearance to view classified material, the request would have appeared to be routine, but the Congressman was unceremoniously denied all access to view the documents, and the White House wouldn't even give an excuse as to why he was barred.

I just can't believe they're going to deny a member of Congress the right of reviewing how they plan to conduct the government of the United States after a significant terrorist attack, DeFazio told the Oregonian.

We're talking about the continuity of the government of the United States of America, DeFazio says. I would think that would be relevant to any member of Congress, let alone a member of the Homeland Security Committee. Maybe the people who think there's a conspiracy out there are right, DeFazio concluded. These new powers have now been handed over to President Obama, allowing him, along with a body of councilors personally selected by him, to declare martial law without there necessarily being a genuine national emergency, greasing the skids for U.S. troops and National Guard to conduct domestic policing of the American people.

In October 2008, Northcom, a Unified Combatant Command of the United States military based out of Peterson AFB, Colorado Springs, was assigned the 3rd.

Infantry Division's 1st Brigade Combat Team returning from Iraq. An alarming September 8 Army Times report which was later denied after it sparked controversy stated that the troops would be used by Northcom to deal with civil unrest and crowd control? in the aftermath of a national emergency. The Obama executive order states that governors will help advise the feds on National Guard, homeland defense, and civil support activities. The fact that the order further blurs the lines between state and federal power, as well as greasing the skids for more military involvement in domestic affairs has stoked fears that Obama may be laying the groundwork for his promised national civilian security force.

Conservatives and libertarians responded to the announcement by expressing their suspicion that Obama is preparing to give governors their marching orders in targeting anti-government? types that have long been characterized as a terrorist threat by the feds in numerous reports stretching back over a decade. There is a definite purpose to this, wrote one commenter on the popular Free Republic website. Is this the initial steps toward a domestic Civilian Security Force each state, as called for by the fascisti during the campaign? It will be coordinated at the state level, under the authority of DHS and DOD and assorted agencies. The provision will be made for it to be federalized? in an emergency, as is the National Guard.

This is a concrete step toward eliminating the independent authority and dissolving the sovereignty of the several States. It lays the groundwork for the end of the United States as a Republic, she adds.

Others warn that Obama could be preparing to cancel elections under the justification of a national emergency, a fear that was often expressed when Bush was in office but one that never materialized.

However, the executive order clearly represents another assault on Posse Comitatus, the 1878 law that
bars the military from exercising domestic police
powers, which was temporarily annulled by the 2006
John Warner National Defense Authorization Act before parts of it were later repealed.

CHAPTER 7: FEMA DEATH CAMPS

A bill has been introduced in the U.S. House of Representatives called the National Emergency Centers Act or HR 645. This bill, if passed into law, will direct the Secretary of Homeland Security to establish national emergency centers otherwise known as FEMA camp facilities on military installations. (Note: This bill was passed in 2009.) This is an incredibly disturbing piece of legislation considering that the powers that be have already set in motion an agenda to setup a nationwide martial law apparatus through U.S. Northern Command and the Department of Homeland Security.

Apparently, the fusion centers, militarized police, surveillance cameras and a domestic military command is not enough. Even though we know that detention facilities are already in place, they now want to legalize the construction of FEMA camps on military installations using the ever-popular excuse that the facilities are for the purposes of a national emergency. With the phony debt-based economy getting worse and worse by the day, the possibility of civil unrest is becoming a greater threat to the establishment. One need only look at Iceland, Greece, and other nations for what might happen in the United States next.

With this in mind, it appears as if these so-called national emergency centers will be used in a national emergency but only if the national emergency requires large groups of people to be rounded up and detained. If that isn't the case, than why have these national emergency facilities been built on military installations?

A leaked U.S. Army document prepared for the Department of Defense contains shocking plans for political activists? to be pacified by PSYOP officers into developing an appreciation of U.S. policies while detained in prison camps inside the United States.

The document, entitled FM 3-39.40 Internment and Resettlement Operations (PDF) was originally released on a restricted basis to the DOD in February 2010, but has now been made public.

The manual outlines policies for processing detainees into internment camps both globally and inside the United States. International agencies like the UN and the Red Cross are named as partners in addition to domestic federal agencies including the Department of Homeland Security and FEMA.

The document makes it clear that the policies apply within U.S. territory and involve, DOD support to U.S. civil authorities for domestic emergencies, and for designated law enforcement and other activities, including man-made disasters, accidents, terrorist attacks and incidents in the U.S. and its territories.

Aside from enemy combatants and other classifications of detainees, the manual includes the designation of civilian internees, in other words citizens who are detained for, security reasons, for protection, or because he or she committed an offense against the detaining power.

Once the detainees have been processed into the internment camp, the manual explains how they will be re-educated, with a particular focus on targeting political dissidents, into expressing support for U.S. policies.

The re-education process is the responsibility of the Psychological Operations Officer, whose job it is to design PSYOP products that are designed to pacify and acclimate detainees or DCs to accept U.S. I/R facility authority and regulations, according to the document.

The manual lists the following roles that are designated to the PSYOP team.

Identifies malcontents, trained agitators, and political leaders within the facility who may try to organize resistance or create disturbances.

Develops and executes indoctrination programs to reduce or remove antagonistic attitudes.

Identifies political activists.

Provides loudspeaker support (such as administrative announcements and facility instructions when necessary).

Helps the military police commander control detainee and DC populations during emergencies.

Plans and executes a PSYOP program that produces an understanding and appreciation of U.S. policies and actions.

Remember, this is not restricted to insurgents in Iraq who are detained in prison camps – the manual makes it clear that the policies also apply within U.S. territory under the auspices of the DHS and FEMA.

The historical significance of states using internment camps to re-educate detainees is the fact that it is almost exclusively practiced by repressive and dictatorial regimes like the former Soviet Union and Stalinist regimes like modern day North Korea.

We have exhaustively documented preparations for the mass internment of citizens inside America, but this is the first time that language concerning the re-education of detainees, in particular political activists, has cropped up in our research.

In 2009, the National Guard posted a number of job opportunities looking for Internment/Resettlement Specialists to work in civilian internee camps within the United States.

In December last year it was also revealed that Halliburton subsidiary KBR is seeking sub-contractors to staff and outfit emergency environment camps located in five regions of the United States.

In 2006, KBR was contracted by Homeland Security to build detention centers designed to deal with ?an emergency influx of immigrants into the U.S, or the rapid development of unspecified ?new programs? that would require large numbers of people to be interned.

Rex 84, short for Readiness Exercise 1984, was established under the pretext of a mass exodus of illegal aliens crossing the Mexican/US border, the same pretense used in the language of the KBR request for services.

During the Iran-Contra hearings in 1987, however, it was revealed that the program was a secretive scenario and drill developed by the federal government to suspend the Constitution, declare martial law, assign military commanders to take over state and local governments, and detain large numbers of American citizens determined by the government to be national security threats.

Under the indefinite detention provision of the National Defense Authorization Act, which was signed by Barack   Obama on New Year's Eve, American citizens can be kidnapped and detained indefinitely without trial.

Intel Hub Note: This U.S. Army document is extremely important to read and understand. This is an open call for government agents to literally pacify the resistance through a massive psyop program involving reeducation camps.

Rex 84: FEMA's Blueprint for Martial Law in America
We are dangerously close to a situation where ~ if the American people took to the streets in righteous indignation or if there were another 9/11 ~ a mechanism for martial law could be quickly implemented and carried out under REX 84.

The Cheney/Bush administration had a plan which would accommodate the detention of large numbers of American citizens during times of emergency.

The plan is called REX 84, short for Readiness Exercise 1984. Through Rex-84 an undisclosed number of concentration camps were set in operation throughout the United States, for internment of dissidents and others potentially harmful to the state.

The Rex 84 Program was originally established on the reasoning that if a "mass exodus" of illegal aliens crossed the Mexican/US border, they would be quickly rounded up and detained in detention centers by FEMA.

Existence of the Rex 84 plan was first revealed during the Iran-Contra Hearings in 1987, and subsequently reported by the Miami Herald on July 5, 1987 "These camps are to be operated by FEMA should martial law need to be implemented in the United States and all it would take is a presidential signature on a proclamation and the attorney general's signature on a warrant to which a list of names is attached."

And there you have it ~ the real purpose of FEMA is to not only protect the government but to be its principal vehicle for martial law.

This is why FEMA could not respond immediately to the Hurricane Katrina disaster ~ humanitarian efforts were no longer part of its job description under the Department of Homeland Security.

It appears Hurricane Katrina also provided FEMA with an excuse to dry run its unconstitutional powers in New Orleans, rounding up refugees (now called evacuees) and relocating them in various camps. Some evacuees are being treated as internees by FEMA, writes former NSA employee Wayne Madsen.

Reports continue to come into WMR that evacuees from New Orleans and Acadiana [the traditional twenty-two parish Cajun homeland] who have been scattered across the United States are being treated as 'internees' and not   dislocated American citizens from a catastrophe". We are dangerously close to a situation where ~ if the American people took to the streets in righteous indignation or if there were another 9/11 ~ a mechanism for martial law could be quickly implemented and carried out under REX 84.

Be forewarned, the administration will stop at nothing to preserve their power and their ongoing neocon misadventure and they have currently proposed having executive control over all the states National Guard troops in a national emergency.

Governor Tom Vilsack of Iowa, called the proposal "one step away from a complete takeover of the National Guard, the end of the Guard as a dual-function force that can respond to both state and national needs."

The provision was tucked into the House version of the defense bill without notice to the states, something Vilsack said he resented as much as the proposal itself. Under the provision, the president would have authority to take control of the Guard in case of " a serious natural or manmade disaster, accident or catastrophe" in the United States. Do remember to the administration ~ the Mob at the Gates that they truly fear is not terrorists but, instead, the people demanding the truth.

REX 84 AND FEMA

MINDFULLY, 2004 - There over 800 prison camps in the United States, all fully operational and ready to receive prisoners. They are all staffed and even surrounded by full-time guards, but they are all empty. These camps are to be operated by FEMA should martial law need to be implemented in the United States and all it would take is a presidential signature on a proclamation and the attorney general's signature on a warrant to which a list of names is attached.

The Rex 84 Program was established on the reasoning that if a "mass exodus" of illegal aliens crossed the Mexican/US border, they would be quickly rounded up and detained in detention centers by FEMA.

Rex 84 allowed many military bases to be closed down and to be turned into prisons.

Operation Cable Splicer and Garden Plot are the two sub programs which will be implemented once the Rex 84 program is initiated for its proper purpose. Garden Plot is the program to control the population. Cable Splicer is the program for an orderly takeover of the state and local governments by the federal government.

FEMA is the executive arm of the coming police state and thus will head up all operations. The Presidential Executive Orders already listed on the Federal Register also are part of the legal framework for this operation.

The camps all have railroad facilities as well as roads leading to and from the detention facilities. Many also have an airport nearby. The majority of the camps can house a population of 20,000 prisoners. Currently, the largest of these facilities is just outside of Fairbanks, Alaska. The Alaskan facility is a massive mental health facility and can hold thousands of people.

FEMA CONCENTRATION CAMPS: Locations and Executive Orders

Iconoclast, on December 7th, 2010

There over 800 prison camps in the United States, all fully operational and ready to receive prisoners. They are all staffed and even surrounded by full-time guards, but they mostly empty. These camps are to be operated by FEMA (Federal Emergency Management Agency) should Martial Law need to be implemented in the United States and all it would take is a presidential signature on a proclamation and the attorney general's signature on a warrant to which a list of names is attached. The Rex 84 Program was established on the reasoning that if a ?mass exodus? of illegal aliens crossed the Mexican/US border, they would be quickly rounded up and detained in detention centers by FEMA. Rex 84allowed many military bases to be closed down and to be turned into prisons.

Operation Cable Splicer and Garden Plot are the two sub programs which will be implemented once the Rex 84 program is initiated for its proper purpose. Garden Plot is the program to control the population. Cable Splicer is the program for an orderly takeover of the state and local governments by the federal government. FEMA is the executive arm of the coming police state and thus will head up all operations. The Presidential Executive Orders already listed on the Federal Register also are part of the legal framework for this operation.

The camps all have railroad facilities as well as roads leading to and from the detention facilities. Many also have an airport nearby. The majority of the camps can house a population of 20,000 prisoners. Currently, the largest of these facilities is just outside of Fairbanks, Alaska. The Alaskan facility is a massive mental health facility and can hold approximately 2 million people.

Halliburton Subsidiary Gets Contract to Add Temporary Immigration D – NY Times.

Now you realize it's not a thing of conspiracy theorists, it's mainstream news. Let's review the justification for any actions taken... Executive Orders associated with FEMA that would suspend the Constitution and the Bill of Rights. These Executive Orders have been on record for nearly 30 years and could be enacted by the stroke of a Presidential pen:

EXECUTIVE ORDERS:

EO 10990 allows the government to take over all modes of transportation and control of highways and seaports.

EO 10995 allows the government to seize and control the communication media.

EO 10997 allows the government to take over all electrical power, gas, petroleum, fuels, and minerals.

EO 10998 allows the government to seize all means of transportation, including personal cars, trucks, or vehicles of any kind and total control over all highways, seaports, and waterways.

EO 10999 allows the government to take over all food resources and farms.

EO 11000 allows the government to mobilize civilians into work brigades under government supervision.

EO 11001 allows the government to take over all health, education, and welfare functions.

EO 11002 designates the Postmaster General to operate a national registration of all persons.

EO 11003 allows the government to take over all airports and aircraft, including commercial aircraft.

EO 11004 allows the Housing and Finance Authority to relocate communities, build new housing with public funds, designate areas to be abandoned, and establish new locations for populations.

EO 11005 allows the government to take over railroads, inland waterways, and public storage facilities.

EO 11051 specifies the responsibility of the Office of Emergency Planning and gives authorization to put all Executive Orders into effect in times of increased international tensions and economic or financial crisis.

EO 11310 grants authority to the Department of Justice to enforce the plans set out in Executive Orders, to institute industrial support, to establish judicial and legislative liaison, to control all aliens, to operate penal and correctional institutions, and to advise and assist the President.

EO 11049 assigns emergency preparedness function to federal departments and agencies, consolidating 21 operative Executive Orders issued over a fifteen-year period.

EO 11921 allows the Federal Emergency Preparedness Agency to develop plans to establish control over the mechanisms of production and distribution, of energy sources, wages, salaries, credit, and the flow of money in U.S. financial institution in any undefined national emergency. It also provides that when a state of emergency is declared by the President, Congress cannot review the action for six months. The Federal Emergency Management Agency has broad powers in every aspect of the nation.

General Frank Salzedo, chief of FEMA's Civil Security Division stated in a 1983 conference that he saw FEMA's role as a new frontier in the protection of individual and governmental leaders from assassination, and of civil and military installations from sabotage and/or attack, as well as prevention of dissident groups from gaining access to U.S. opinion, or a global audience in times of crisis.

FEMA's powers were consolidated by President Carter.

National Security Act of 1947 allows for the strategic relocation of industries, services, government, and other essential economic activities, and to rationalize the requirements for manpower, resources, and production facilities.

1950 Defense Production Act gives the President sweeping powers over all aspects of the economy.

Act of August 29, 1916 authorizes the Secretary of the Army, in time of war, to take possession of any transportation system for transporting troops, material, or any other purpose related to the emergency.

International Emergency Economic Powers Act enables the President to seize the property of a foreign country or national. These powers were transferred to FEMA in a sweeping consolidation in 1979.

So, where exactly are these camps?

ALABAMA

Opelika– Military compound either in or very near town.

Aliceville – WWII German POW camp – capacity 15,000

Ft. McClellan (Anniston)– Opposite side of town from Army Depot

Maxwell AFB (Montgomery)– Civilian prison camp established under Operation Garden Plot, currently operating with support staff and small inmate population.

Talladega – Federal prison satellite camp.

ALASKA

Wilderness – East of Anchorage. No roads, Air & Railroad access only. Estimated capacity of 500,000. Projection: forced labor camp.

Elmendorf AFB – Northeast area of Anchorage – far end of base. Garden Plot facility, as well as a Circular Disposed Antenna Array (CDAA) used for High Frequency Direction Finding (HFDF) covering 2 to 32 Megahertz that is operated by the United States Navy.

Eielson AFB– Southeast of Fairbanks. Operation Garden Plot facility.

Ft. Wainwright– East of Fairbanks

ARIZONA

Ft. Huachuca – Airbase– 20 miles from Mexican border, 30 miles from Nogales Rex '84 facility.

Pinal County – on the Gila River– WWII Japanese detention camp. May be renovated.

Yuma County – Colorado River- Site of former Japanese detention camp (near proving grounds). This site was completely removed in 1990 according to some reports.

Phoenix – Federal Prison Satellite Camp– Main federal facility expanded.

Florence– WWII prison camp NOW RENOVATED, OPERATIONAL with staff & 400 prisoners, operational capacity of 3,500.

Wickenburg– Airport is ready for conversion, total capacity unknown.

Davis – Monthan AFB (Tucson)– Fully staffed and presently holding prisoners!!

Sedona– site of possible UN base.

ARKANSAS

Ft. Chaffee (near Fort Smith, Arkansas)- Has new runway for aircraft, new camp facility with cap of 40,000 prisoners.

Pine Bluff Arsenal– This location also is the repository for B-Z nerve agent, which causes sleepiness, dizziness, stupor; admitted use is for civilian control.

Jerome – Chicot/Drew Counties- site of WWII Japanese camps

Rohwer – Descha County– site of WWII Japanese camps.

Blytheville AFB- Closed airbase now being used as camp. New wooden barracks have been constructed at this location. Classic decorations – guard towers, barbed wire, high fences.

Berryville – FEMA facility located east of Eureka Springs off Hwy. 62. [near Tyson's property.]

Omaha– Northeast of Berryville near Missouri state line, on Hwy 65 south of old wood processing plant on a dirt road that leads to a toxic waste dump. Possible crematory facility.

CALIFORNIA

Vandenburg AFB– Rex 84 facility, located near Lompoc & Santa Maria on Hwy 1, close to Hwy 101.

Internment facility is located near the oceanside, close to Space Launch Complex #6, also called ?Slick Six?. The launch site has had ?a flawless failure record? and is rarely used.

Norton AFB– (closed base) now staffed with UN according to some sources.

Tule Lake– area of ?wildlife refuge?, accessible by unpaved road, just inside Modoc County.

Fort Ord– Now called Presidio of Monterey – Closed in 1994, this facility is now an urban warfare training center for US and foreign troops and may have some ? P.O.W. – C.I.? enclosures.

Twentynine Palms Marine Base – Birthplace of the infamous ?Would you shoot American citizens?? Quiz. New camps being built on back 40.

Oakdale– Rex 84 camp capable of holding at least 20,000 people. 90 mi east of San Francisco on Hwy 120.

Terminal Island – (Long Beach)– located next to naval shipyards operated by ChiCom shipping interests. Federal prison facility located here. Possible deportation point.

Ft. Irwin – view 2 from higher up – view 3 from higher up with Edwards AFB, George AFB (Closed?) and MCLB Barstow and Ft. Irwin in perspective – Ft. Irwin is a FEMA facility near Barstow. This base is designated inactive but has staffed camp. The surrounding support from Edwards AFB, George AFB, and MCLB Barstow would indicate this is a high importance facility. MCLB Barstow has an interesting mark on its helicopter pad, which looks suspiciously like an Iron Cross. Check it out. Another view. Irwin is a remote mountain region south of Death Valley National Monument. Designated as inactive, there is a camp at this facility approximately 30 miles from I-15 in Barstow. McClellan AFB(Closed) – facility capable for 30,000 – 35,000.

Sacramento – Army Depot– The Sacramento Army Depot (SAAD) was a U.S. Army support facility that operated as a repair center for high-tech military hardware, such as night vision goggles, electronic circuit boards, and radium-dial instrumentation. The 1988 Base Closure and Realignment Commission closed Sacramento Army Depot. On March 3, 1995, the Depot officially closed.

In the Fall of 1994 Packard Bell, the computer company whose plant in Northridge was damaged by an earthquake decided to relocate a 3,000-employee assembly plant and distribution center at the Depot. As of April 1996, Packard Bell had 3,500 employees working at its Depot facility (down from 5,000 in August 1995) and in February 1998 there were 3,100 employees, in October 1998 3,400 employees. This is the only Packard Bell manufacturing plant in the U.S. In mid-2000, Packard Bell NEC, Inc. announced it would shut down all manufacturing operations by year's end and lay off 1,400 of its 1,550 workers at the former Sacramento Army Depot.

Mather AFB – Road to facility is blocked off by cement barriers and a stop sign. Sign states area is restricted; as of 1997 there were barbed wire fences pointing inward, a row of stadium lights pointed toward an empty field, etc. Black boxes on poles may have been cameras. Closer examinations reveal black helicopters, and a whole lot more activity than a ?closed? base should have. Still more planes and cars at the supposedly closed base including two very large seemingly unmarked jets prepping for takeoff. Also, visible was a whole fleet of red tipped planes, which I am told are firefighting planes.

COLORADO

Trinidad– WWII German/Italian camp being renovated.

Granada – Prowers County – Camp Amache WWII Japanese internment camp.

Ft. Carson– Along route 115 near Canon City

CONNECTICUT, DELAWARE

No data available.

DELAWARE

No data available.

FLORIDA

Avon Park– Air Force gunnery range, Avon Park has an on-base ?correctional facility? which was a former WWII detention camp.

Camp Krome – view 2– DOJ detention/interrogation center, Rex 84 facility.

Eglin AFB – This base is over 30 miles long, from Pensacola to Hwy 331 in De Funiak Springs. High-capacity facility, presently manned and populated with some prisoners. fighter jets occupying the tarmac, more fighters, fighters and bombers, along with a very unusual swept wing aircraft.

GEORGIA

Ft. Benning– Rex 84 Program Emergency custodial facility east of Columbia, near Georgia/Alabama state line. Prisoners may be brought in via Lawson Army airfield Oglethorpe, Macon County– FEMA facility 5 miles from Montezuma, 3 miles from Oglethorpe, on west side of Hwy 49. No staff or prisoners yet.

Ft. McPherson – US Force Command – Multiple reports that this will be the national headquarters and coordinating center for foreign/UN troop movement and detainee collection.

Ft. Gordon – West of Augusta - They seem to like Base-ball and track a LOT at Ft. Gordon. There's a strangely shaped building which is reminiscent of the masonic symbol. To the east of the field, is an odd symbology on the ground. Noticeable also is a fleet of black cars in the north parking lot. There is another fleet of black cars in the south parking lot. There is also a strangely shaped complex of buildings that appears to look like Da Vinci's model of the human body, only depicted as an old Atari 2600 graphic, it appears.

Camilla – Mitchell County, south of Albany- FEMA facil-ity on Mount Zion road approximately 5.7 miles south of Camilla. From Camilla, take Hwy 19 south, go 5.4 miles from 37/19 Junction to Mount Zion Road, turn left (east) on Mount Zion Road. Not manned or staffed yet.

Hawkinsville – Wilcox County– Five miles east of town, fully manned and staffed but no prisoners. Located on fire road 100/Upper River Road

Abbeville– South of Hawkinsville on US route 129; south of town off route 280 near Ocmulgee River. FEMA facility is staffed but without prisoners.

McRae – Telfair County– 1.5 miles west of McRae on Hwy 23 (8th St). Facility is on Irwinton Avenue off 8th St., manned & staffed – no prisoners.

Fort Gillem – South side of Atlanta – FEMA designated detention facility.

Fort Stewart – Savannah area – FEMA designated detention facility

HAWAII

Halawa Heights area – Crematory facility located in hills above city. Area is marked as a state department of health laboratory.

Barbers Point NAS – There are several military areas that could be equipped for detention / deportation.

Honolulu – Detention transfer facility at the Honolulu airport similar in construction to the one at Will Rogers World Airport. (Federal Transfer Centers look like pentagon-shaped building where airplanes can taxi up to).

IDAHO

Minidoka/Jerome Counties– WWII Japanese-American internment facility possibly under renovation.

Clearwater National Forest – Near Lolo Pass– Just miles from the Montana state line near Moose Creek, this unmanned facility is reported to have a nearby airfield.

ILLINOIS

Marseilles – Located on the Illinois River off Interstate 80 on Hwy 6. It is a relatively small facility with a cap of 1400 prisoners. Though it is small it is designed like prison facilities with barred windows, but the real smoking gun is the presence of military vehicles. Being located on the Illinois River it is possible that prisoners will be brought in by water as well as by road and air. This facility is approximately 75 miles west of Chicago. National Guard training area nearby.

Scott AFB – Barbed wire prisoner enclosure reported to exist just off-base. More info needed, as another facility on-base is believed to exist.

Pekin – This Federal satellite prison camp is also on the Illinois River, just south of Peoria. It supplements the federal penitentiary in Marion, which is equipped to handle additional population outside on the grounds.

Chanute AFB – Rantoul, near Champaign/Urbana– This closed base had WWII – era barracks that were condemned and torn down, but the medical facility was upgraded, and additional fencing put up in the area. More info needed.

Marion – Federal Penitentiary and satellite prison camp inside Crab Orchard National Wildlife Refuge. Manned, staffed, populated fully.

Greenfield – Two federal correctional

?satellite prison camps? serving Marion – populated as above.

Shawnee National Forest – Pope County– This area has seen heavy traffic of foreign military equipment and troops via Illinois Central Railroad, which runs through the area. Suspected location is unknown but may be close to Vienna and Shawnee correctional centers, located 6 mi. west of Dixon Springs.

Savanna Army Depot– NW area of state on Mississippi River.

Lincoln, Sheridan, Menard, Pontiac, Galesburg– State prison facilities equipped for major expansion and close or adjacent to highways & railroad tracks.

Kankakee – Abandoned industrial area on west side of town (Rt.17 & Main) designated as FEMA detention site. Equipped with water tower, incinerator, a small train yard behind it and the rear of the facility is surrounded by barbed wire facing inwards.

INDIANA

Indianapolis / Marion County – Beech Grove– Amtrak railcar repair facility (closed); controversial site of a major alleged detention / processing center. Although some sources state that this site is a ?red herring?, photographic and video evidence suggests otherwise.

This large facility contains large 3–4-inch gas mains to large furnaces (crematoria??), helicopter landing pads, railheads for prisoners, Red/Blue/Green zones for classifying/processing incoming personnel, one-way turnstiles, barracks, towers, high fences with razor wire, etc. Personnel with government clearance who are friendly to the patriot movement took a guided tour of the facility to confirm this site. (see video above) This site is located next to a closed refrigeration plant facility.

Ft. Benjamin Harrison– Located in the northeast part of Indianapolis, this base has been decommissioned from ?active? use but portions are still ideally converted to hold detainees. Helicopter landing areas still exist for prisoners to be brought in by air, land & rail.

Crown Point – Across street from county jail, former hospital. One wing presently being used for county work-release program, 80% of facility still unused. Possible FEMA detention center or holding facility.

Camp Atterbury - Facility is converted to hold prisoners and boasts two active compounds presently configured for minimum security detainees. Located just west of Interstate 65 near Edinburgh, south of Indianapolis.

Terre Haute – Federal Correctional Institution, Satellite prison camp and death facility. Equipped with crematoria reported to have a capacity of 3,000 people a day. FEMA designated facility located here.

Fort Wayne – This city located in Northeast Indiana has a FEMA designated detention facility, accessible by air, road, and nearby rail.

Kingsbury – This ?closed? military base is adjacent to a state fish & wildlife preserve. Part of the base is converted to an industrial park, but the southern portion of this property is still used. It is bordered on the south by railroad and is staffed with some foreign-speaking UN troops. A local police officer who was hunting and camping close to the base in the game preserve was accosted, roughed up, and warned by the English-speaking unit commander to stay away from the area. It was suggested to the officer that the welfare of his family would depend on his ?silence?. Located just southeast of LaPorte.

Jasper-Pulaski Wildlife Area– Youth Corrections farm located here. Facility is closed but is still staffed and being ?renovated?. Total capacity unknown.

Grissom AFB– This closed airbase still handles a lot of traffic and has a state-owned prison compound on the southern part of the facility.

UNICOR

Jefferson Proving Ground – Southern Indiana – This facility was an active base with test firing occurring daily. Portions of the base have been opened to create an industrial park, but other areas are still highly restricted. A camp is located downrange. Facility is equipped with an airfield and has a nearby rail line.

Newport – Army Depot– VX nerve gas storage facility. Secret meetings were held here in 1998 regarding the addition of the Kankakee River watershed to the Heritage Rivers Initiative.

Hammond– large enclosure identified in FEMA-designated city.

IOWA

No data available.

KANSAS

Leavenworth – US Marshal's Fed Holding

Facility, US Penitentiary, Federal Prison Camp.

McConnell Air Force Base – Federal death penalty facility.

Concordia – WWII German POW camp used to exist at this location but there is no facility there at this time.

Ft. Riley – Just north of Interstate 70, airport, near city of Manhattan.

El Dorado – Federal prison converted into forced-labor camp, UNICOR industries.

Topeka – 80 acres has been converted into a temporary holding camp.

KENTUCKY

Ashland – Federal prison camp in Eastern Kentucky near the Ohio River.

Louisville – FEMA detention facility, located near restricted area US naval ordnance plant. Military airfield located at facility, which is on south side of city.

Lexington – FEMA detention facility, National Guard base with adjacent airport facility.

Manchester – Federal prison camp located inside Dan Boone National Forest.

Ft. Knox – Detention center, possibly located near Salt River, in restricted area of base. Local patriots advise that black Special Forces & UN gray helicopters are occasionally seen in area.

Land Between the Lakes- This area was declared a UN biosphere and is an ideal geographic location for detention facilities. Area is an isthmus extending out from Tennessee, between Lake Barkley on the east and Kentucky Lake on the west. Just scant miles from Fort Campbell in Tennessee.

LOUISIANA

Ft. Polk – This is a main base for UN troops & personnel, and a training center for the disarmament of America.

Livingston – WWII German/Italian internment camp being renovated?; halfway between Baton Rouge and Hammond, several miles north of Interstate 12.

Oakdale – Located on US route 165 about 50 miles south of Alexandria; two federal detention centers just southeast of Fort Polk.

MAINE

Houlton – Camp is reported to be a WWII German internment camp in Northern Maine, off US Route 1 but the location and the existence of this camp is still unconfirmed.

MARYLAND and DC

Ft. Meade – Halfway between the District of Criminals and Baltimore.

Ft. Detrick– Biological warfare center for the NWO, located in Frederick.

MASSACHUSETTS

Camp Edwards / Otis AFB – Cape Cod – This inactive base is being converted to hold many New Englander patriots. Capacity unknown.

Ft. Devens– Active detention facility. More data needed.

MICHIGAN

Camp Grayling– Michigan National Guard base has several confirmed detention camps, classic setup with high fences, razor wire, etc. Guard towers are very well-built, sturdy. Multiple compounds within larger enclosures. Facility deep within forest area.

Sawyer AFB – Upper Peninsula– south of Marquette – No data available.

Bay City – Classic enclosure with guard towers, high fence, and close to shipping port on Saginaw Bay, which connects to Lake Huron. Could be a deportation point to overseas via St. Lawrence Seaway.

Southwest – possibly Berrien County – FEMA detention center.

Lansing – FEMA detention facility.

MINNESOTA

Duluth – Federal prison camp facility.

Camp Ripley – new prison facility.

MISSISSIPPI

These sites are confirmed hoaxes.

Hancock County – NASA test site De Soto National Forest. ?These two supposed camps in Mississippi do not exist. Members of the Mississippi Militia have checked these out on more than one occasion beginning back when they first appeared on the Internet and throughout the Patriot Movement.? – Commander D. Rayner, Mississippi Militia

MISSOURI

Richards - Gebaur AFB– located in Grandview, near K.C.MO. A very large internment facility has been built on this base, and all base personnel are restricted from coming near it.

Ft. Leonard Wood – Situated in the middle of Mark Twain National Forest in Pulaski County. This site has been known for some UN training, also home to the US Army Urban Warfare Training school ?Stem Village?.

Warsaw – Unconfirmed report of a large concentration camp facility.

MONTANA

Malmstrom AFB – UN aircraft groups stationed here, and possibly a detention facility.

NEBRASKA

Scottsbluff – WWII German POW camp (renovated?).

Northwest, Northeast corners of state – FEMA detention facilities – more data needed.

South Central part of state– Many old WWII sites – some may be renovated.

NEVADA

Elko – Ten miles south of town.

Wells – Camp is located in the O'Neil basin area, 40 miles north of Wells, past Thousand Springs, west off Hwy 93 for 25 miles.

Pershing County – Camp is located at I-80 mile marker 112, south side of the highway, about a mile back on the county road and then just off the road about 3/4mi.

Winnemucca – Battle Mountain area- at the base of the mountains.

Nellis Air Force Range – Northwest from Las Vegas on Route 95. Nellis AFB is just north of Las Vegas on Hwy 604.

Stillwater Naval Air Station – east of Reno . No additional data.

NEW HAMPSHIRE / VERMONT

Northern New Hampshire – near Lake Francis. No additional data.

NEW JERSEY

Ft. Dix / McGuire AFB – Possible deportation point for detainees. Lots of pictures taken of detention compounds and posted on Internet, this camp is well-known. Facility is now complete and ready for occupancy.

NEW MEXICO

Ft. Bliss – This base actually straddles Texas state line. Just south of Alamogordo, Ft. Bliss has thousands of acres for people who refuse to go with the ?New Order?.

Holloman AFB (Alamogordo)- Home of the German Luftwaffe in Amerika; major UN base. New facility being built on this base, according to recent visitors. Many former USAF buildings have been torn down by the busy and rapidly growing German military force located here.

Fort Stanton – currently being used as a youth detention facility approximately 35 miles north of Ruidoso, New Mexico. Not a great deal of information concerning the Lordsburg location.

White Sands Missile Range – Currently being used as a storage facility for United Nations vehicles and equipment. Observers have seen this material brought in on the White Sands rail spur in Oro Grande New Mexico about thirty miles from the Texas, New Mexico Border.

NEW YORK

Ft. Drum – two compounds: Rex 84 detention camp and FEMA detention facility.

Albany – FEMA detention facility.

Otisville – Federal correctional facility, near Middletown.

Buffalo – FEMA detention facility.

NORTH CAROLINA

Camp Lejeune / New River Marine Airfield – facility has renovated, occupied WWII detention compounds and mock city that closely resembles Anytown, USA.

Fort Bragg - Special Warfare Training Center. Renovated WWII detention facility.

Andrews – Federal experiment in putting a small town under siege. Began with the search/ hunt for survivalist Eric Rudolph. No persons were allowed in or out of town without federal permission and travel through town was highly restricted. Most residents compelled to stay in their homes. Unregistered Baptist pastor from Indiana visiting Andrews affirmed these facts.

NORTH DAKOTA

Minot AFB – Home of UN air group. More data needed on facility.

OHIO

Camp Perry – Site renovated, once used as a POW camp to house German and Italian prisoners of WWII. Some tar paper covered huts built for housing these prisoners are still standing. Recently, the construction of multiple 200-man barracks have replaced most of the huts.

Cincinnati, Cleveland, Columbus – FEMA detention facilities. Data needed.

Lima – FEMA detention facility. Another facility located in/near old stone quarry near Interstate 75. Railroad access to property, fences etc.

OKLAHOMA

Tinker AFB (OKC) – All base personnel are prohibited from going near civilian detention area, which is under constant guard.

Will Rogers World Airport – FEMA's main processing center for west of the Mississippi. All personnel are kept out of the security zone. Federal prisoner transfer center located here (A pentagon-shaped building where airplanes can taxi up to).

El Reno – Renovated federal internment facility with CURRENT population of 12,000 on Route 66.

McAlester – near Army Munitions Plant property – former WWII German / Italian POW camp designated for future use.

Ft. Sill (Lawton) – Former WWII detention camps. More data still needed.

OREGON

Sheridan – Federal prison satellite camp northwest of Salem. FEMA detention center.

Josephine County – WWII Japanese internment camp ready for renovation.

Umatilla – New prison spotted.

PENNSYLVANIA

Allenwood – Federal prison camp located south of Williamsport on the Susquehanna River. It has a current inmate population of 300 and is identified by William Pabst as having a capacity in excess of 15,000 on 400 acres.

Indiantown Gap Military Reservation – located north of Harrisburg. Used for WWII POW camp and renovated by Jimmy Carter. Was used to hold Cubans during Mariel boat lift.

Camp Hill – State prison close to Army depot. Lots of room, located in Camp Hill, Pa.

New Cumberland Army Depot – on the Susquehanna River, located off Interstate 83 and Interstate 76.

Schuylkill Haven – Federal prison camp, north of Reading.

SOUTH CAROLINA

Greenville – Unoccupied youth prison camp; total capacity unknown.

Charleston – Naval Reserve & Air Force base, restricted area on naval base.

SOUTH DAKOTA

Yankton – Federal prison camp Black Hills National Forest – north of Edgemont, southwest part of state. WWII internment camp being renovated.

TENNESSEE

Ft. Campbell - Next to Land Between the Lakes; adjacent to airfield and US Alt. 41.

Millington – Federal prison camp next door to Memphis Naval Air Station.

Crossville – Site of WWII German / Italian prison camp is renovated; completed barracks and behind the camp in the woods is a training facility with high tight ropes and a rappelling deck.

Nashville – There are two buildings built on State property that are definitely built to hold prisoners. They are identical buildings – side by side on Old Briley Parkway. High barbed wire fence that curves inward.

TEXAS

Austin – Robert Mueller Municipal airport has detention areas inside hangars.

Bastrop – Prison and military vehicle motor pool. Eden – 1500 bed privately run federal center. Currently holds illegal aliens.

Ft. Hood (Killeen) – Newly built concentration camp, with towers, barbed wire etc., just like the one featured in the movie Amerika. Mock city for NWO shock-force training. Some footage of this area was used in Waco: A New Revelation.

Reese AFB (Lubbock) – FEMA designated detention facility.

Sheppard AFB – in Wichita Falls just south of Ft. Sill, OK– FEMA designated detention facility.

North Dallas – near Carrolton– water treatment plant, close to interstate and railroad.

Mexia – East of Waco 33mi –WWII German facility may be renovated.

Amarillo – FEMA designated detention facility

Ft. Bliss (El Paso) – Extensive renovation of buildings and from what patriots have been able to see, many of these buildings that are being renovated are being surrounded by razor wire.

Beaumont / Port Arthur area– hundreds of acres of federal camps already built on large-scale detention camp design, complete with the double rows of chain link fencing with razor type concertina wire on top of each row. Some (but not all) of these facilities are currently being used for low-risk state prisoners who require a minimum of supervision.

Ft. Worth– Federal prison under construction on the site of Carswell AFB.

UTAH

Millard County – Central Utah– WWII Japanese camp. (Renovated?)

Ft. Douglas – This ?inactive? military reservation has a renovated WWII concentration camp.

Migratory Bird Refuge – West of Brigham City– contains a WWII internment camp that was built before the game preserve was established.

Cedar City – east of city– no data available.

Wendover – WWII internment camp may be renovated.

Skull Valley – southwestern Camp William property-east of the old bombing range. Camp was accidentally discovered by a man and his son who were rabbit hunting; they were discovered and apprehended. SW of Tooele.

VIRGINIA

Ft. A.P. Hill (Fredericksburg) – Rex 84 / FEMA facility. Estimated capacity 45,000.

Petersburg – Federal satellite prison camp, south of Richmond.

WEST VIRGINIA

Beckley – Alderson – Lewisburg – Former WWII detention camps that are now converted into active federal prison complexes capable of holding several times their current populations. Alderson is presently a women's federal reformatory.

Morgantown – Federal prison camp located in northern WV, just north of Kingwood.

Mill Creek – FEMA detention facility.

Kingwood – Newly built detention camp at Camp Dawson Army Reservation. More data needed on Camp Dawson.

WASHINGTON

Seattle/Tacoma – SeaTac Airport– fully operational federal transfer center

Okanogan County – Borders Canada and is a site for a massive concentration camp capable of holding hundreds of thousands of people for slave labor. This is probably one of the locations that will be used to hold hard core patriots who will be held captive for the rest of their lives.

Sand Point Naval Station – Seattle – FEMA detention center used actively during the 1999 WTO protests to classify prisoners.

Ft. Lewis / McChord AFB – near Tacoma – This is one of several sites that may be used to ship prisoners overseas for slave labor.

WISCONSIN

Ft. McCoy – Rex 84 facility with several complete interment compounds.

Oxford – Central part of state– Federal prison & satellite camp and FEMA detention facility.

WYOMING

Heart Mountain – Park County N. of Cody– WWII Japanese internment camp ready for renovation.

Laramie – FEMA detention facility

Southwest – near Lyman– FEMA detention facility

East Yellowstone – Manned internment facility – Investigating patriots were apprehended by European soldiers speaking in an unknown language. Federal government assumed custody of the persons and arranged their release.

OTHER LOCATIONS IN THE UNITED STATES

There are many other locations not listed above that are worthy of consideration as a possible detention camp site, but due to space limitations and the time needed to verify, could not be included here. Virtually all military reservations, posts, bases, stations, & depots can be considered highly suspect (because it is ?federal? land). Also fitting this category are ? Regional Airports? and ?International Airports? which also fall under federal jurisdiction and have limited-access areas. Mental hospitals, closed hospitals & nursing homes, closed military bases, wildlife refuges, state prisons, toxic waste dumps, hotels and other areas all have varying degrees of potential for being a detention camp area. The likelihood of a site being suspect increases with transportation access to the site, including airports/airstrips, railheads, navigable waterways & ports, interstate and

US highways. Some facilities are ?disguised? as industrial or commercial properties, camouflaged or even wholly contained inside large buildings (Indianapolis) or factories. Many inner-city buildings left vacant during the deindustrialization of America have been quietly acquired and held, sometimes retrofitted for their new uses.

CANADA

Our Canadian friends tell us that virtually all Canadian military bases, especially those north of the 50th Parallel, are all set up with concentration camps. Not even half of these can be listed, but here are a few sites with the massive land space to handle any population:

Suffield CFB – just north of Medicine Hat, less than 60 miles from the USA.

Primrose Lake Air Range – 70 miles northeast of Edmonton.

Wainwright CFB – halfway between Medicine Hat and Primrose Lake.

Ft. Nelson – Northernmost point on the BC Railway line.

Ft. McPherson – Very cold territory ~ NW Territories.

Ft. Providence – Located on Great Slave Lake.

Halifax – Nova Scotia –Dept. of National

Defense reserve. And others.

OVERSEAS LOCATIONS

Guaynabo, Puerto Rico – Federal prison camp facility. Capacity unknown.

Guantanamo Bay, Cuba – US Marine Corps Base – Presently home to 30,000 Mariel Cubans and 40,000 Albanians. Total capacity unknown.

CHAPTER 8: N.W.O. PLANS FOR US

Hollywood director and documentary film maker Aaron Russo has gone in-depth on the astounding admissions of Nick Rockefeller, who personally told him that the elite's ultimate goal was to create a micro-chipped population and that the war on terror was a hoax, Rockefeller having predicted an event that would trigger the invasions of Iraq and Afghanistan eleven months before 9/11. Rockefeller also told Russo that his family's foundation had created and bankrolled the women's liberation movement in order to destroy the family and that population reduction was a fundamental aim of the global elite. Russo is perhaps best known for producing Trading Places starring Eddie Murphy but was more recently in the spotlight for his expose of the criminal run for profit Federal Reserve System, the documentary

Currently undergoing more treatment in his fight against cancer (He lost his battle with cancer on August 24/2007), Russo made time for a sit-down interview with radio host and fellow documentary film maker Alex Jones in which he dropped bombshell after bombshell on what Rockefeller had told him about the direction the world was being steered towards by the global elite.

After his popular video Mad as Hell was released and he began his campaign to become Governor of Nevada, Russo was noticed by Rockefeller and introduced to him by a female attorney. Seeing Russo's passion and ability to affect change, Rockefeller set about on a subtle mission to recruit Russo into the elite.

During one conversation, Rockefeller asked Russo if he was interested in joining the Council on Foreign Relations (CFR), but Russo rejected the invitation, saying he had no interest in enslaving the people to which Rockefeller coldly questioned why he cared about the serfs.

"I used to say to him what's the point of all this", states Russo, — you have all the money in the world you need, you have all the power you need, what's the point, what's the end goal?‖ to which Rockefeller replied (paraphrasing), —The end goal is to get everybody chipped, to control the whole society, to have the bankers and the elite people control the world. Rockefeller even assured Russo that if he joined the elite his chip would be specially marked so as to avoid undue inspection by the authorities.

Russo states that Rockefeller told him, eleven months before 9/11 happened there was going to be an event and out of that event we were going to invade Afghanistan to run pipelines through the Caspian sea, we were going to invade Iraq to take over the oil fields and establish a base in the Middle East, and we'd go after Chavez in Venezuela. Rockefeller also told Russo that he would see soldiers looking in caves in Afghanistan and Pakistan for Osama bin Laden and that there would be an —Endless war on terror where there's no real enemy and the whole thing is a giant hoax, so that the government could take over the American people,‖ according to Russo, who said that Rockefeller was cynically laughing and joking as he made the astounding prediction.

In a later conversation, Rockefeller asked Russo what he thought women's liberation was about. Russo's response that he thought it was about the right to work and receive equal pay as men, just as they had won the right to vote, caused Rockefeller to laughingly retort, "You're an idiot! Let me tell you what that was about, we the Rockefeller's funded that, we funded women's lib, we're the ones who got all of the newspapers and television the Rockefeller Foundation."

Rockefeller told Russo of two primary reasons why the elite bankrolled women's lib, one because before women's lib the bankers couldn't tax half the population and two because it allowed them to get children in school at an earlier age, enabling them to be indoctrinated into accepting the state as the primary family, breaking up the traditional family model. This revelation dovetails previous admissions on behalf of feminist pioneer Gloria Steinem that the CIA bankrolled Ms. Magazine as part of the same agenda of breaking up traditional family models. Rockefeller was often keen to stress his idea that —the people have to be ruled by an elite and that one of the tools of such power was population reduction, that there were —too many people in the world, and world population numbers should be reduced by at least half.

One issue which has spiraled out of control of the elite according to Rockefeller's conversations with Russo, is the Israel-Palestine conflict, with serious thinking at one stage revolving around the bizarre notion of giving Israeli citizens one million dollars each and relocating them all in the state of Arizona. Rockefeller also told Russo that his family's foundation had created and bankrolled the women's liberation movement in order to destroy the family and that population reduction was a fundamental aim of the global elite. Russo is perhaps best known for producing Trading Places starring Eddie Murphy but was more recently in the spotlight for his exposé of the criminal run for profit Federal Reserve System, the documentary

While undergoing treatment in his fight against cancer (a fight he lost on August 24, 2007), Russo made time for a sit-down interview with radio host and fellow documentary film maker Alex Jones in which he dropped bombshell after bombshell on what Rockefeller had told him about the direction the world was being steered towards by the global elite.

After his popular video Mad As Hell was released and he began his campaign to become Governor of Nevada, Russo was noticed by Rockefeller and introduced to him by a female attorney. Seeing Russo's passion and ability to affect change, Rockefeller set about on a subtle mission to recruit Russo into the elite.

During one conversation, Rockefeller asked Russo if he was interested in joining the Council on Foreign Relations (CFR), but Russo rejected the invitation, saying he had no interest in —enslaving the people to which Rockefeller coldly questioned why he cared about the serfs. I used to say to him what's the point of all this, states Russo, you have all the money in the world you need, you have all the power you need, what's the point, what's the end goal to which Rockefeller replied (paraphrasing), The end goal is to get everybody chipped, to control the whole society, to have the bankers and the elite people control the world.‖ Rockefeller even assured Russo that if he joined the elite his chip would be specially marked so as to avoid undue inspection by the authorities.

Russo states that Rockefeller told him, eleven months before 9/11 happened there was going to be an event and out of that event we were going to invade Afghanistan to run pipelines through the Caspian sea, we were going to invade Iraq to take over the oil fields and establish a base in the Middle East, and we'd go after Chavez in Venezuela.

Rockefeller also told Russo that he would see soldiers looking in caves in Afghanistan and Pakistan for Osama bin Laden and that there would be an — endless war on terror where there's no real enemy and the whole thing is a giant hoax, so that the government could take over the American people,‖ according to Russo, who said that Rockefeller was cynically laughing and joking as he made the astounding prediction.

In a later conversation, Rockefeller asked Russo what he thought women's liberation was about. Russo responded that he thought it was about the right to work and receive equal pay as men, just as they had won the right to vote, causing Rockefeller to laughingly retort, "You're an idiot! Let me tell you what that was about. We Rockefeller's funded that, we funded women's lib, we're the ones who got all of the newspapers and television – the Rockefeller Foundation."

Rockefeller told Russo of two primary reasons why the elite bankrolled women's lib. First, before women's lib the bankers couldn't tax half the population and second, it allowed them to get children in school at an earlier age, enabling them to be indoctrinated into accepting the state as the primary family, breaking up the traditional family model.

This revelation dovetails previous admissions on behalf of feminist pioneer Gloria Steinem that the CIA bankrolled Ms. Magazine as part of the same agenda of breaking up traditional family models.

Rockefeller was often keen to stress his idea that — the people have to be ruled‖ by an elite and that one of the tools of such power was population reduction, that there were —too many people in the world,‖ and world population numbers should be reduced by at least half.

One issue which has spiraled out of control of the elite according to Rockefeller's conversations with Russo, is the Israel-Palestine conflict, with serious thinking at one stage revolving around the bizarre notion of giving Israeli citizens one million dollars each and relocating them all in the state of Arizona.

CHAPTER 9:
AMERICA – AS THE
GRIP TIGHTENS

"Once upon a time, in Old America, there was pride in the workmanship of American Made[60]". American Small towns overflowed with creation. Manufacturing, tools, paper mills, steel mills, machinery of all kinds were everywhere. We didn't have militarized police breaking down doors without knocking and killing innocent citizens. Doctors came to your house; the President didn't advise those in need to sit in an emergency room for hours. Medical bills didn't bankrupt entire families. Medicines were affordable. People and hometown businesses filled Small town America. Walmart and everything "made in China" was not the largest employer in the nation. The elderly didn't need to apply for jobs; bagging groceries or as Home Depot Associates to make ends meet. Schools were not centers of social engineering, teaching alternative lifestyles, or the intricacies of putting a condom on a banana. Children were permitted the joy of being a child and not arrested for zero tolerance schemes, thought up by some mindless educators in Washington.

It used to be that a man working in a blue-collar job

like a mill or auto plant could see his son becoming an engineer, a doctor, or scientist. Now, children, have their careers being mapped out by social engineers. College costs are unheard of high with grants and loans being canceled. Kids don't work at paper routes anymore, or at odd jobs. These are filled now by the elderly, unemployed parents, or immigrants legal or illegal. Preparing for a world of continual warfare doesn't need math skills, spelling, or reading skills. Many graduating can't do simple math, read a newspaper, or discuss anything of value. They no longer have any idea of history. Today, a compliant, obedient, passive work force, needs early intervention and training in obedience. It takes a village to raise a mindless idiot.

Whose fault is it? Do we point the finger at Parents? Do we point the finger at government? Who allowed this mess of indoctrinating children into stupidity? Teachers are no longer called to the work of teaching. Most are interested in a paycheck or benefits. Without hesitation children are prescribed mind-altering drugs all without research. There was not always the fear of the "stranger danger", Amber Alerts, the daily bad news or selfishness inducing advertisements. Streets and parks were alive with the laughter of children at play, carnivals, swimming, picnics, concerts in the park, fishing, building forts.

Once upon a time in Old America a man working in a mill, or auto plant etc., could see his son becoming an engineer, a doctor, or scientist. Today's child has his/

her career being mapped out in school by social engineers. College costs are out of sight, with various grants and loans being eliminated. Youngsters no longer work at paper routes, or at odd jobs. These are being done by unemployed parents or immigrants.

Those being prepared for a world of Forever War – or placement in the local widget factory; don't need math skills, spelling, or reading abilities. Thus, many graduating today, can't do simple math (watch what happens when the computers go down in a store), read a newspaper, or discuss a work of literature. Many have no idea of our history, and think the civil war was the Watts Riots. Try asking your fourth grader to look up a word in the dictionary or write a short story.

The fault of this rests with parents/citizens – who have allowed this madness of indoctrinating their children into stupidity. Teachers (change agents) are only interested in a paycheck or retirement benefits. They are not about to rock the boat. Citizens on the other hand, without a murmur, have their children prescribed mind altering drugs, without the least bit of research. Because some bovine drone threatens them – they bleat and obey. Would that we had some zero-tolerance addressing the corruption in Foggy Bottom – or in the robbery of war, with billions gone missing. Meantime, the offspring of the moneyed/well connected, receive the best of private school educations to prepare them for their secure positions of future hucksters, industry hacks etc.

Once upon a time in Old America there was no stranger danger, Amber Alerts, or daily fear advertisements. True we had Duck and Cover, a silly ass routine of Bert the Turtle, advising us to duck under a desk, to avoid the aftermath of an Atomic Bomb. At age six, I had enough sense to see the lunacy in this, and received a monthly unsatisfactory' in deportment, because I wouldn't participate in acting the fool. Today I imagine I'd be arrested.

Once upon a time in Old America the streets and parks were alive with the laughter of children at play. Small town America had its fireworks, parades, carnivals, swimming hole, family picnics, concerts in the park, fishing, building forts etc. Today the streets are silent and echoing on a summer's eve. Video games and mindless TV programming have created a generation of lumpkins. Except in a rare instance, I don't recall a classroom filled with doughy – dullard overweight children. But then we had no fast-food restaurants, or additive saturated foods, when I was growing up. To this day, I have never eaten at a McSlop fast food joint (WHY DO THAT?).

Citizens today have been propagandized and programed to enslaved consumerism. I can't imagine that my parents would have paid hundreds of dollars for sneakers, or designer clothing , so that I could fit in with the other kids at school. _TV was my teacher far into the night – it taught me to buy everything within sight' – this is today's mantra. Imagine robbing

your children, by sitting them down in front of something called Sponge Bob(or whatever) or violent video
games?

We are for the most part kept ill informed as to the true
state of our nation.

Millions are losing their jobs and homes. One state
or region has no idea of what is occurring elsewhere.
Detroit looks like Beirut – with its downtown echoing with abandoned hotels, train stations, and rusted
auto plants. The steel mills and textile plants of Middle
America – the South (never modernized), were allowed
to rust into oblivion – with few realizing the implications. In times of crisis, we could never prepare for war.

Once upon a time in Old America there were real grand-
mas with aprons and flowered dresses. Women didn't
feel the need to resort (TV conditioning) to liposuc-
tion, face lifts, breast implants etc. Our votes weren't
hijacked by computers with no paper trail. True, there
have always been the robber barons exploiting the
workers, shooting down strikers (looking for a decent
wage), and crooked politicians, only too willing to sell
out their constituents. The difference today is that
these robber barons and corporate hucksters; hold the
most strategic positions in government (from the Defense Dept to the regulatory agencies).

Lobbyists for industry now determine legislation. Government (politicians) for the most part, are nothing

more than props. No matter the party in power, one can observe, that they are about feathering their own nests, serving their corporate owners, or holding tedious hearings, that result in nothing but filling time. Anything done for the citizen is by pure accident.

And now in the New America we can see that our infrastructure, utilities, water, and vast holdings of real estate are being sold out to foreign interests. Rest assured, that all these supposed protected areas (parks – timber – minerals – grasslands – etc.) are mere collateral for our massive debt. I suspect, that under the guise of paperless ID, we will next be ordered to be chipped (much like pets). In the days of slavery this was called branding – the chip is merely updated branding. One must keep track of one's human resources on a plantation.

Today the streets are silent and empty because the kids - and the adults - are lost in video games and mindless TV. Citizens today have been programed and enslaved by consumerism. We are ignorant about the true state of affairs. Millions have lost and are losing their jobs and homes. Millions are at home, out of work and have given up looking. Detroit looks like Beirut with its downtown echoing with abandoned hotels, train stations, and rusted auto plants. "The steel mills and textile plants of Middle America were allowed to rust into oblivion with few realizing the implications." Our votes weren't hijacked by computers with no paper trail. The difference today is that today's robber barons and corporate hucksters; hold the strategic positions in government. Lobbyists for industry determine legislation.

No matter which party is in power, they are busy about feathering their own nests, serving their corporate owners, or holding tedious hearings, that result in nothing but filling time. Anything done for the citizen is purely accidental. New America - our infrastructure, utilities, water, and vast holdings of real estate - is being sold to foreign interests. All these supposed protected areas - parks, timber, minerals, grasslands - are mere collateral for our massive debt.

I project that under the cover of paperless ID's, we will next be ordered to be chipped, like pets. In the days of slavery this was called branding – the chip is merely updated branding for the new slaves.

Summary: An interview with Mr. Sea regarding New World Order plans for the U.S. and its citizens

In the spring of 1997, Senior Editor, Professor Ian Stewart, met with "Mr. Sea" - real name withheld - to discuss what he has learned first-hand about the coming persecution at the hands of the New World Order operatives. With a seven-inch thick portfolio filled with photographs, news articles, correspondence, etc., Mr. Sea revealed disturbing information about New World Order efforts to destroy and enslave America.

"Mr. Sea, a committed Christian, is a former inspector for the Joint Chiefs of Staff and the Department of Defense, with 31 years of federal service in the military, nine with the Department of Defense, including two years with the Air Staff. He's a holder of the Bronze Star, the Purple Heart, the Defense Meritorious Service Medal, three awards of the Joint Service Medal, all of the Vietnamese awards, as well as the Joint Meritorious Unit Medal. When he retired a few years ago, he was awarded the Secretary of Defense Civilian Service Medal. He's been around the world, to 31 countries on four continents, and speaks five languages. Mr. Sea spoke of the coming American Holocaust of the Government's plans for dealing with the non-New World Order Acolytes. He spoke of the infrastructure that has already been set up to incarcerate and execute Americans, and the locations of the facilities that will be used for these purposes, all with photographs, leaving little to the imagination. The infrastructure is set up. There are at least more than 130 concentration camps[61] quietly modified facilities which have sprung up and continue to spring up across the country, seemingly devoid of activity, yet requiring strange accoutrements such as barbed wire-topped fencing (with the tops turned inward) and helicopter windsocks. Most have good logistical supportability, with major highways and railroad transport facilities adjacent to the sites. These facilities, many in remote areas across our country, are set up to become concentration/detention camps, complete with gas chambers, for resisters and dissidents. Generally speaking, they're set up for dissenters who will not go along with the New World Order. The resisters are gun owners who refuse to give up their weapons; the dissidents are Christians, Patriots and Constitutionalists. These camps are set up. I've seen many of them."

"On August 6, 1994, I toured the Amtrak Railcar Repair Facility at Beech Grove, Indianapolis, Indiana. There are at least ten maintenance barns at this facility, covering 129 acres, with two separate fences with the tops leaning inward. The windows of several buildings have been bricked up. Hence, you have three levels of security for Amtrak repair barns! There are three helicopter 25-knot aviation windsocks (which aren't the correct ones to use for chemical spills which require 10-knot windsocks). There are high security NSA-style people turnstiles, and high intensity/security lighting for 24-hour operation. The box car (gas chamber) building fence is marked with special RED/BLUE Zone signs]. This corresponds to the mission of the RED/BLUE Lists which surfaced in June and July of 1996. Under martial law, this will become a death camp. They're only going to handle category one and two (RED and BLUE) people there. This box car facility will be used for execution. One of the barns is large enough to put four box cars into. There are powered vents on the top of the barn to vent the gas out of the building after the box cars have been fumigated. All of the buildings have newly installed six-inch gas pipes and furnaces installed in all railroad barns.

FEMA has allocated $6 million to make the walls and roofs of the buildings airtight. Under martial law, this facility could be immediately used as an SS-style termination gas chamber.

"On January 27, 1995, The Indianapolis News ran an article titled, Amtrak Lays off 212 at Beech Grove: 170 Lose Jobs at Maintenance Center Today.

Why perform $6 million worth of renovations, and then lay off 212 people? Because the people doing the final executions will not be Americans. Thus, the slots of the 212 will be filled with non-Americans. They'll hire foreigners for this cappo task. Cappo - chief' in Italian - was the title of the trustee prisoners who actually killed many Jews for the SS butchers at Dachau, and at other Nazi crematoria across Europe. The news article also said, ...hopes the yard may be able to solicit work repairing private train cars, and perhaps subway cars from Washington, DC, or other urban areas.' The repairing of private trains is a dead giveaway to death cars! The article went on to say, Late last year, Congress ordered Amtrak to spend at least $5.9 million patching holes in the roof and fixing masonry on the walls of the giant machine sheds at Beech Grove.' These buildings have been sealed.' They're airtight. The facility is constructed to allow gas to be blown into all the buildings via the newly installed, two-story, not air heating furnaces."

Next, Mr. Sea elaborated on the two categories the RED and BLUE Lists, and what they mean: "The RED List is for pick-up and execution before unobtrusive preparations for martial law are initiated. The BLUE List is also for execution, but at a later date within six weeks of martial law declaration. There are no re-education' plans for either category just execution. When you get picked up on a RED pick-up, they'll take you from your home at night -- probably around 4 a.m. -- and put you in a black van, then drive you to a helicopter waiting to fly you to an intermediate point.

There, you'll be loaded onto a big 64-passenger CH-47 Chinook helicopter black, unmarked and illegally operating under the Treaty on Open Skies. Then they'll fly you to one of 38 cities where you'll board a 747, 737, or 727. "You may be taken straight to a temporary detention facility. When you're RED listed, you'll be taken to a red camp. Then you'll be executed.

"At some point, martial law will be declared. (Martial law is when the writ of Habeas Corpus -- to have a trial by jury -- is suspended. Instead, of going to the judge, you go straight to jail for a limited time,) I suspect there will be a major outage, or some other crisis which will be the reason to declare martial law. At this point, the BLUE listed people will be picked up. At that time, the country will be regionalized into ten regions, which are already designated by FEMA. Be advised that it has been proven (in Wyoming and at least one other location) that the black choppers have state-of-the-art radio (RF) frequency wideband jammers and can jam cell phones and CBs while they're executing black operations missions (i.e., in your area). This means that your cell phone could be jammed just before and/or during any action against you.

"In June of 1996, an FBI agent got hold of the Region Three BLUE List (from a CIA agent), and found his own name on it, and those of several others he knew in Virginia. The Regional BLUE List stated that the names on the BLUE List would be picked up within six weeks of the actual martial law declaration.' This parallels the Nazi RED/BLUE List policy almost to the letter. The parallel Nazi plan was published by Heinz Hohne in his 1966 book, The Story of the Nazi SS: The Order of the Death's Head.

"People say, It won't work.' But it will work if the 300,000 Soviet troops which are ALREADY HERE can get the guns. The name of the game is to blackball the people to get the guns...make the militia look bad, make guns look bad, make everybody give up their guns. Once they get your gun, they've got you, UNLESS you've got the angel of the Lord at your door. If you've got the angel of the Lord out there protecting you, it's another story.

"The ones doing all of this are operating out of the highest places in the Federal Government. They're co-operating with _spirit guides and mediums' and using astrology and numerology. The spirit guides are telling them what to do, and the entire thing is being orchestrated at the highest spiritual levels. Every base has been covered. They've thought of everything. If you notice, they often do things on the 13th of the month. The President does a lot of things on the 13th.

"Who will be doing the actual picking up? Foreign _cops' (United Nations Internal Security Forces). Over 30 foreign military bases under the United Nations flag are already set up in the US all with the approval of special appointees in high Federal positions. These bases are already manned with over ONE MILLION troops from Russia, Poland, Germany, Belgium, Turkey, Great Britain, Nicaragua, and Asian countries. Why are they here? Because unlike our own troops --many of which along with the Guard and Reserve of 24 states are being deployed overseas -- will have no qualms about firing on U.S. citizens when the time comes. There are more than 2,000 Russian tanks, military trucks, and chemical warfare vehicles just outside Gulfport, Mississippi. They began arriving in January of 1994. There are 180 foreign troops at Fort Reilly which was confirmed to me by a Brigadier General. There are 300 who came into the Birmingham, Alabama airport on a big white Russian cargo plane on December 13, 1995. As of 1995, there were 10,000 plus foreign troops at Fort Chafee, Arkansas reportedly making preparations for 20,000 detainees.' This is going on all over the country. German troops are known to be at Holloman Air Force Base in New Mexico, Wright-Patterson Air Force Base in Ohio, and Fort Hood, Texas. Chinese troops are known to be at the Long Beach Naval Station in California. There's not going to be some future event when the invading troops are going to show up.

They're already here! When martial law is implemented, these foreign U.N. troops will be policing our country, carrying out the plans of the New World Order.

What can we do to stop the NWO?

Knowledge is Power, Spread the Knowledge

There is a growing awareness in America and England. The Awareness of the Big Question. There is no sentence, there is no paragraph, there is no reading that will serve to answer that question. What is holding them off right now is the fact that the masses do not fully trust the government to represent the people. And the Patriot groups are growing stronger.

These are the things that are preventing the New World Order planners. They are desperate trying to find ways to diffuse the information coming out against them. They are also looking for ways to disarm the citizens. We are now aware of the struggle, and it cannot simply be hidden again. It is something that is happening.

What can we do?

Each person becoming aware adds to the power of the

masses. People who are not aware are simply uninvolved bodies, asleep, human meat on the hoof, as they would say, and they contribute nothing of value to ending the crisis, or to its resolution. They are simply there, like a tree, like a bush. The bushes and the trees in battle do not play much of a part. They may be used for people to hide behind, or they may be slaughtered during the war, but the bush and the tree are not motivated to do anything in regard to a battle. These people may be used, they may be slaughtered or victimized, but they do not know why, and they do not know what they are doing if they do anything. They do not know what is going on.

This is not the first time that writing, the pen, is being used to win a victory. Thomas Paine and his writings helped to win the Revolutionary War, helped to turn the tide against the supporters of Britain, and in favor of the Colonies and their independence.

People do not despair. There is a huge number of people whose interests lie in preserving the good life for each other, and those who would enslave the masses are very few, and though they have many who work for them, they do so more out of fear than out of desire. They do not desire to enslave their fellow man but will do so because they are afraid that if they do not, they themselves will suffer greater ills.

As the people awaken, they'll begin to recognize who their true enemies and oppressors are, and those who fill positions in-between will come to recognize the power of the people as greater than that of the masters, and their allegiance will change, not to support the masters, but to work for the masses.

It is perhaps too early to say, but it appears that the masses in the end, will remain in charge and regain the power that has been recognized to be theirs by the Constitution. Those who would destroy the Constitution and enslave the masses will be out of luck and will have exposed themselves for what they are.

Knowledge is power.

CHAPTER 10: FOUNDING FATHERS OF THE FUTURE GENERATIONS

A war of information is underway. We are involved in a war of information, but, it is not a shooting war, yet. It may yet become a shooting war. The information that is spread to awaken the masses may be enough to ward off war, and to keep the masses free from oppression. Changes occur over decades and they occur so slowly and so subtly, sometimes people are not aware of the changes until they look back. You are the Founding Fathers of the Future Generations. The threat doesn't necessarily result in oppression. People do not heed or watch and become aware of the threats may become oppressed. Continue to be awakened and alarmed, but you appreciate the moments where you are free, and use those moments to help preserve future freedom, to help defuse that threat that might otherwise impinge on your future. That you think not only of your freedom, but also of the freedom of your children and the future generations. You must think not just of your freedom, but also of the freedom of your children and the future generations, for you are the founding fathers of the future generations. You are the heroes of tomorrow's generations, and if you fail these future generations, these children of your children may curse you, and rightly so. Be aware of the dangers and threats to the freedom and security of your own and future generations[62], and to do what is within your own power to make sure that these freedoms are passed from generation to generation; that every moment there are powers who would deny these freedoms, who would seek to gain their own power and freedom at the expense of others.

No one is free until all are free. These powers seek to gain more freedom for themselves by denying freedom to others. Make sure that excessive greed for power or personal freedom at the expense of others is not expressed in such a way as to deny your freedom and the freedom of your children and their children. When someone presents something that they say is good for you and your children, look at it and question whether this is just another trick to deny your freedoms, or it indeed has something to offer your children and your children's children.

Does the Proposed Health care System pose a threat? If the health care programs requires that all citizens in the country have a health card, does this not constitute a national identity card? And is this not the way of tracking individuals, much like the license plates on cars, and is this really the main purpose of this so-called health care plan that is being promoted with such fanfare?, or is it truly a humanitarian effort to make sure that everyone has proper health care? Why does this health care plan force people to have a choice only of the one particular type of medicine? Is there not a right for people to have a choice of the types of medical help they wish? Must everyone come under the domain of the American Medical Association? Is this health care plan promoted by these entities or in their behalf? There are many questions about this health care plan that need to be explored further, and fortunately, there are many people now who are giving this another look, so that it is not going to be jammed down the throats of Americans without examination. The same appears to be happening to the North American Free Trade Agreement treaty. It is also examined by many segments of society. These two programs, and no doubt many others, are part of the scenario for promoting the New World Order (Global Governance). The gun law efforts also being part of that program of imposing the New World Order on America and is likewise finding certain resistance.

All of these things together suggests that the New World Order isn't coming like a blazing locomotive but is chugging very slowly and having considerable difficulty in reaching its destination. Perhaps this is a good sign that it is being examined carefully from a lot of different angles so that it does not simply push out the Constitution and impose itself without the masses having any idea of what is going on. There is at least, resistance to the idea of simply allowing a NWO to seat itself upon the masses without their invitation and understanding of what is happening. People questioning: "What is going on here anyway?" That resistance is an act of preserving our freedoms. There is no harm at this time of asking: "What is this all about?" These questions may one day be forbidden, even as they were once forbidden in Poland and behind the Iron Curtain in many of the other countries where you could not question authority for it was forbidden, and you had simply to obey or be exterminated.

You still have freedoms because of the Constitution that is the law of the land, because of the customs of the land, of the nation, of the culture. Are you willing to risk your freedoms to try something different simply because some authorities advocate a New World Order with rousing voices? What indeed is this New World Order? Is it not the same thing as the old-world efforts of a few to gain control of the many? For if it is, we have heard the tune many times before, and it is no different from many of the old-world orders that have existed down through history, except today it is larger in its scope and have many subtle methods of reaching its goal.

The Constitution, the Bill of Rights, all of these things could be thrown out and new rules, new laws, even dictatorial or tyrannical laws could well be introduced to govern the masses. This would all be legal. Few people recognize that the Federal Reserve was set up illegally and the loans from the Federal Reserve to the country were set up to make loans and notes that were not real money and there are a few people who see it as a legal way out of the so-called national debt; that the country declare a national moratorium against the national debt because it was not legally made.

The Federal Reserve note is but a note not based on the U.S dollar, the treasury note being the correct dollar or monetary unit and the Federal Reserve note being created improperly because it was done unconstitutionally could be seen as a reason to void the debt that has been created. Some understand this clearly. Could any the influence necessary to turn this around and prevent the privately owned Federal Reserve Bank from foreclosing on this nation?

It would be much easier for people to go along with the authorities on everything that is promoted. For then there is no threat of resistance or counter-action. People who go along to get along too often find themselves ensnared in the slaughterhouse, in enslavement, imprisonment and this has been so throughout the history of humanity. People do not have to go along just to get along without being aware of the dangers involved in your actions, sometimes a stich in time can alter the outcome.

People must become more and more aware of what is happening in their world, to take the right actions. War is occurring over the capture and containment of the souls of humanity and the war is being fought with ideas and concepts and information. It could, at a future time, include weapons, and the weapons may be used in the future to wipe out segments of society, if the ideas of today are not used properly in this battle for control of the minds of people, for as people seek to understand, they may turn to the wrong sources, if your voice isn't present, if your information isn't available.

As you spread the information, spread opportunities for others to see a different side of the picture. Don't think you have nothing to say.

CHAPTER 11: THE DARK FORCES PREMATURELY CELEBRATING

The Dark Forces may be celebrating victory prematurely. We are living in extremely interesting times of great significance to the human existence and to the history of humanity on Earth. Whether humanity moves into this new age as a master and slaves or whether humanity throws off the potential tyrant to prevent becoming slaves. The next few years will determine this. It is intended that the New World Order be well established soon, but within that period it is possible that Freedom, particularly in the United States, may need a more solid foundation to let humans move into the new millennium with dignity and freedoms still intact.

Could it be that the planet Earth, itself is being prepared for a kind of rejuvenation? people must cease passing the blame and cease patting themselves on the back and begin to open their eyes. End listening to the forked tongue of the Beast, to cease being hypnotized by the electronic programmer and the printed words and to tune into Christ. Look toward each other and cease finding the flaw in each other.

When everything else is crashing down remember that the One God is near and all around you. God is available for all people to cry out to during any time or anywhere they may be. This is something that may be of great importance to you in coming times when there are moments of uncertainty or confusion. When the world around you appears to be deteriorating or falling apart, keep in mind that the one thing which is always stable is that God is everywhere present, in all things in all places. He never changes.

Hollywood is doing it again. This time it's the terminal endgame for the planet. The blockbuster 2012 was released in movie theatres on November 12th. The trailer for this movie paints an ominous planetary apocalypse where man's greatest fear or in some cases denial becomes a final reality. In much of Judaic-Christian apocalyptic literature, end time scenarios paint a future of literal cleansing of the earth by fire and desolation. As 2012 highlights the ferocity of devastating earthquakes which creates record-breaking tsunamis coupled with Category 6 hurricanes which push global temperatures into bizarre fluctuations - the planet tether-totters as it writhes in cosmic agony as a pregnant woman in the labor pain of childbirth. One may argue that predictions of how the world would end have been around for thousands of years. We can read summations of this based on the opening of the 7 Seals in the book of Revelation where the Horsemen of the Apocalypse dole out war, famine, plague, and death. Jesus will bring the final doomsday where the "Sun Will Rise in the West" and usher in the Golden Age. It gels with the Mayan definition of the end of time where the next prophesied great cycle will occur on Friday, December 21, 2012.

According to Mayan prophecy it is said that the Sun will be in alignment during the winter solstice perfectly crossing the equatorial plane of the Milky Way. Astronomers and cosmologists agree that the Solar System only enters this plane twice during this Great Cycle' producing this phenomenon called a GALACTIC REVOLUTION. The Mayan Popol Vuh's - the Mayan 'Bible' - prophecy of the end of times is based on the Mayans mathematical and astronomical calculations devising probably the most accurate calendars known to man - even more accurate than the modern Gregorian calendar – showing through extremely accurate observations of the sun, the planets, the stars and the Milky Way galaxy, possessing knowledge concerning the Precession of the Equinoxes, and as they approached the study of prophecy they looked at the periodicity of cycles, especially astronomical ones, and their connection to human events. The Mayan Calendar which was based on a 20-day month with a year, revolving every 20 years, or what is called a Katun (generation) – and each 20 —Katuns was called a —b'ak'tun, and where [13] of these made a Great Cycle (about 5125 years). This Great Cycle ended in December of 2012. But is this all-ancient religious title tattle concerning THE end? Does anyone really know the future for sure?

Traditional Hindu prophecies, as described in the Puranas and other Sanskrit texts, warns us that the world will fall into chaos and degradation where perversity, greed, and conflict, will be rife as described in the following statement: "When deceit falsehood, lethargy, sleepiness, violence, despondency, grief, delusion, fear, and poverty prevail ... when men, filled with conceit, consider themselves equal with the Brahmins...that is the Kali Yuga." Then according to Hindu prophecy, the AVATAR come: "The lord shall manifest Himself as the Kalki Avatar... He will establish righteousness upon the earth and the minds of the people will become as pure as crystal... As a result, the Sat or Krta Yuga (Golden Age) will be established." Like Hindus, Buddhists also believe in a cycle of destruction and creation. Buddha believed his teachings would've disappeared after 500 years because it was in man's nature to follow the ten amoral concepts of theft, violence, murder, lying, evil speaking, adultery, abusive and idle talk, covetousness and ill will, wanton greed, and perverted lust resulting in skyrocketing poverty and the end of the worldly laws of true dharma. A new Buddha called the "Maitreya" will arise to renew the teachings of Buddhism and rediscover the path to Nirvana. Maitreya is believed to currently be residing in the Tusita heaven, where he is awaiting his final rebirth in the world. In Judaic hermeneutic tradition, the end of the world is called the Acharit Hayamim (End of Days). Global

apocalyptic events will destroy the old-world order creating a New Order in which God is universally recognized as the Ruler over everyone and everything. Sages
of the Talmud say: "Let the end of days come", but may
I hope not to live to see them, because they will be filled
with so much conflict, suffering and destruction no
eyes would want to see such devastation.

In Native American prophecy it is said that a great
dwelling place in the heavens shall fall with a great
crash to the earth and it appears as a blue star, and
the earth will rock to and fro. It is also prophesied that
during the end times the earth would be crossed by
iron snakes and stone rivers, (railroads?), and the land
would be criss-crossed by a giant spider's web (free-
ways?), and seas will turn black (oil spills?). Many will
die, but those who understand the prophecies shall live
in the places of the Native American people and be safe.

Science is also facing up to the serious challenges our
planet is undergoing. In a scientific research city in
the heart of Siberia, geophysicists are concerned that
the solar system is moving into a highly charged inter-
stellar energy cloud and these renowned physicists are
trying to make sense of the fact that the earth's mag-
netic field is vanishing. Amongst the vast field of data
are concerns based on empirical scientific research on
solar data; the increasing incidents of earthquakes and
the growing areas of seismic activity; volcanic activity
around Mount St. Helens and a myriad of global issues
which impact on every inhabitant on the earth. Re-

search at the Solar & Heliospheric Observatory opens a fascinating window on the awesome beauty of planet and many skeptics cannot imagine that this wonderful planet including the heavens around us will one day go into meltdown.

Whatever your belief these are the facts, the prophecies and the strands of philosophy which provided the necessary ammunition for all of us to make decisive choices.

I have presented many views, thoughts, and words of many researchers, writers, and speakers from over the globe. I do not say that I favor one over the other. What I do say is that we should have an open mind to all possibilities and be prepared for those who would exert their power of all humanity. There are far too many things that we simply do not know for sure, nor can we know with our present level of understanding. But this one thing stands out: the earth as we know it will end. No one knows for sure when.

And then the New Earth!

Who survives the endgame is anyone's guess.

On a Mundane Plane - On Lake Fork in east Texas, near a little country town called Alba, is a great restaurant with the best food in the area. It is called Tiffany's Restaurant. And My-O-My the pies! Tiffany makes the best pies in the State of Texas. One of the owners is Joe,

Tiffany's husband. (I refuse to mention his last name.) I eat there regularly, and we have many great conversations. Joe is very intelligent - not only about local happenings, but also about the world at large.

On one evening, we were talking about the hundreds of boxcars the government had ordered from China for FEMA Camps that had shackles and Guillotines.

I asked Joe what he thought about that fact?

He grinned and said: Don't take the eff-ing trains!

Nuff said. End of story.

ENDNOTES

---

[1] Revelation 6:8 ESV

[2] http://en.wikipedia.org/wiki/Illuminati

[3] World Population Clock

[4] The Protocols of the Elders of Zion

[5] useless eaters

[6] http://www.scribd.com/doc/7423676

[7] Depopulation Conspiracy Theory

[8] http://www.noiseofthunder.com/articles/2011/4/6/the-oracle-of-the-revolution-thomas-paine.html

[9] http://en.wikipedia.org/wiki/Georgia_Guidestones

[10] http://www.americanthinker.com/articles/2011/04/the_un_and_one_world_worship.html

[11] Agenda 21

[12] http://christianity.about.com/od/biblestorysummaries/p/towerofbabel.htm

[13] http://en.wikipedia.org/wiki/Earth_Charter

[14] http://www.cuttingedge.org/news/n1394.cfm

[15] http://www.principiadiscordia.com/downloads/The_Illuminati_Papers_-_Robert.pdf

[16] 2 Corinthians 11:14

[17] http://en.wikipedia.org/wiki/Congress_of_Vienna

[18] http://www.rense.com/general80/pike.htm

[19] The Invisible Enemy II: Vendetta (Google eBook) - Anthony R. Howard - Jun 25, 2012

[20] The Quest for Truth: Come Now and Let Us Reason Together - Michael Dedivonai - AuthorHouse, Aug 28, 2012

[21] http://www.henrymakow.com/the_united_states_is_a_masonic.html

[22] The Constitutions of the Free-Masons - James Anderson, Benjamin Franklin - Lulu.com, 2008 - This is a new edition of the first Masonic book printed in America, which was originally produced in Philadelphia by Benjamin Franklin in 1734, and was a reprint of a work by James Ander-

son (who is identified as the author in an appendix) printed in London in 1723.This is the seminal work of American Masonry, edited and published by one of the founding fathers, and of great importance to the development of colonial society and the formation of the Republic. The work contains a 40-page history of Masonry: from Adam to the reign of King George I, including, among others, Noah, Abraham, Moses, Solomon, Hiram Abif, Nebuchadnezzar, Augustus Caesar, Vitruvius, King Athelstan the Saxon, Inigo Jones, and James I of England. It is a celebration of the science of Geometry and the Royal Art of Architecture. The work also includes five songs, one of which-"A New Song"-appears in print for the first time and may have been composed by Franklin.

[23] http://www.gwmemorial.org/washingtonTheMason.php

[24] Masons coordinated from nation to nation

[25] The Eye of Providence

[26] Bilderberg Elite Plan Economic Depression

[27] http://www.prisonplanet.com/bilderberg-wants-global-department-of-health-global-treasury.html

[28] The Trilateral Commission: Usurping Sovereignty

[29] http://en.wikipedia.org/wiki/Trilateral_Commission

[30] http://en.wikipedia.org/wiki/David_Rockefeller

[31] http://en.wikipedia.org/wiki/Council_on_Foreign_Relations

[32] http://en.wikipedia.org/wiki/Federal_Reserve_Act

[33] http://en.wikipedia.org/wiki/Edward_M._House

[34] http://en.wikipedia.org/wiki/League_of_Nations

[35] None Dare call it Conspiracy

[36]   http://www.amazon.com/None-Dare-Call-It-Conspiracy/dp/0945001290

[37]   http://www.amazon.com/FDR-my-exploited-father-law/dp/B0006BT4W8

[38] http://www.cfr.org/

[39] http://youtu.be/8yO6NSBBRtY

[40]   http://www.theforbiddenknowledge.com/hardtruth/alternata-tives123.htm

[41]   https://hendersonlefthook.wordpress.com/2014/07/23/the-illu-minati-depopulation-agenda/comment-page-1/

[42] Modern Esoteric: Beyond Our Senses - Brad Olsen - Mar 1, 2014

[43]   https://books.google.com/books?id=72HJAgAAQBAJ&pg=PA190&lpg=PA190&dq=Dr.+Eva+Snead,+San+Francisco+has+one+of+the+highest+cancer+rates+in+the+country&source=bl&ots=Sbh8NrXyl-&sig=Vjycklatdf-NACnza4424UVUJ3w&hl=en&sa=X&ei=rN_XVJrMDIHigwTtw4LQDw&ved=0CCYQ6AEwAQ#v=onepage&q=Dr. Eva Snead, San Francisco has one of the highest cancer rates in the country&f=false

[44] http://educate-yourself.org/nwo/reportironmountain2.shtml

[45]   http://www.google.com/url?sa=t&rct=j&q=&esrc=s&source=web&cd=7&ved=0CEwQFjAG&url=http://costsofwar.org/sites/all/themes/costsofwar/images/Civilian_Death.pdf&ei=seDXVJ7IKIWuggSwn4TQAQ&usg=AFQjCNGZ5F1Rgdc64Kmq67NvVhBcrQV0ng

[46] https://thewhiteroseii.wordpress.com/tag/surveillance/

[47] http://en.wikipedia.org/wiki/Paul_E._Vallely

[48] http://en.wikipedia.org/wiki/Temple_of_Set

[49] http://en.wikipedia.org/wiki/BrainGate

[50] http://en.wikipedia.org/wiki/Sanctions_against_Iraq

[51] http://israelect.com/reference/WillieMartin/AIDS.htm

[52] http://all-natural.com/riley.html

[53] http://en.wikisource.org/wiki/Riegle_Report

[54] Forced Sale of Gas Ingredient to Army

[55]   http://www.theforbiddenknowledge.com/hardtruth/resnick_inter-view_peter_kawaja.htm

[56] Gulf War Registry

[57] http://en.wikipedia.org/wiki/Oklahoma_City_bombing

[58] https://nwoobserver.wordpress.com/2009/page/70/

[59]http://www.washingtonpost.com/blogs/therootdc/post/ron-paul-dennis-kucinich-wont-soon-be-forgotten/2012/05/15/gIQAgJbzRU_blog.html

[60]http://rense.com/general79/oldtime.htm

[61]http://www.apfn.org/apfn/camps.htm

[62]http://www.bibliotecapleyades.net/sociopolitica/master_file/youare-foundingfathers.htm

CREDITS

ENDNOTES

[1] Revelation 6:8 ESV

[2] http://en.wikipedia.org/wiki/Illuminati

[3] World Population Clock

[4] The Protocols of the Elders of Zion

[5] useless eaters

[6] http://www.scribd.com/doc/7423676

[7] Depopulation Conspiracy Theory

[8] http://www.noiseofthunder.com/articles/2011/4/6/the-or-acle-of-the-revolution-thomas-paine.html

[9] http://en.wikipedia.org/wiki/Georgia_Guidestones

[10] http://www.americanthinker.com/articles/2011/04/the_un_and_one_world_worship.html

[11] Agenda 21

[12] http://christianity.about.com/od/biblestorysummaries/p/towerofbabel.htm

[13] http://en.wikipedia.org/wiki/Earth_Charter

[14] http://www.cuttingedge.org/news/n1394.cfm

[15] http://www.principiadiscordia.com/downloads/The_Illu-minati_Papers_-_Robert.pdf

[16] 2 Corinthians 11:14

[17] http://en.wikipedia.org/wiki/Congress_of_Vienna

[18] http://www.rense.com/general80/pike.htm

[19] The Invisible Enemy II: Vendetta (Google eBook) - Anthony R. Howard - Jun 25, 2012

[20] The Quest for Truth: Come Now and Let Us Reason Together - Michael Dedivonai - AuthorHouse, Aug 28, 2012

[21]   http://www.henrymakow.com/the_united_states_is_a_mason-ic.html

[22] The Constitutions of the Free-Masons - James Anderson, Benjamin Franklin - Lulu.com, 2008 - This is a new edition of the first Masonic book printed in America, which was originally produced in Philadelphia by Benjamin Franklin in 1734, and was a reprint of a work by James Anderson (who is identified as the author in an appendix) printed in London in 1723.This is the seminal work of American Masonry, edited and published by one of the founding fathers, and of great importance to the development of colonial society and the formation of the Republic. The work contains a 40-page history of Masonry: from Adam to the reign of King George I, including, among others, Noah, Abraham, Moses, Solomon, Hiram Abif, Nebuchadnezzar, Augustus Caesar, Vitruvius, King Athelstan the Saxon, Inigo Jones, and James I of England. It is a celebration of the science of Geometry and the Royal Art of Architecture. The work also includes five songs, one of which-"A New Song"-appears in print for the first time and may have been composed by Franklin.

[23] http://www.gwmemorial.org/washingtonTheMason.php

[24] Masons coordinated from nation to nation

[25] The Eye of Providence

[26] Bilderberg Elite Plan Economic Depression

[27] http://www.prisonplanet.com/bilderberg-wants-global-department-of-health-global-treasury.html

[28] The Trilateral Commission: Usurping Sovereignty

[29] http://en.wikipedia.org/wiki/Trilateral_Commission

[30] http://en.wikipedia.org/wiki/David_Rockefeller

[31] http://en.wikipedia.org/wiki/Council_on_Foreign_Relations

[32] http://en.wikipedia.org/wiki/Federal_Reserve_Act

[33] http://en.wikipedia.org/wiki/Edward_M._House

[34] http://en.wikipedia.org/wiki/League_of_Nations

[35] None Dare call it Conspiracy

[36]	http://www.amazon.com/None-Dare-Call-It-Conspiracy/dp/0945001290

[37]	http://www.amazon.com/FDR-my-exploited-father-law/dp/B0006BT4W8

[38] http://www.cfr.org/

[39] http://youtu.be/8y06NSBBRtY

[40]	http://www.theforbiddenknowledge.com/hardtruth/alternatatives123.htm

[41]	https://hendersonlefthook.wordpress.com/2014/07/23/the-illuminati-depopulation-agenda/comment-page-1/

[42] Modern Esoteric: Beyond Our Senses - Brad Olsen - Mar 1, 2014

[43]	https://books.google.com/books?id=72HJAgAAQBAJ&pg=PA190&lpg=PA190&dq=Dr.+Eva+Snead,+San+Francisco+has+one+of+the+highest+cancer+rates+in+the+country&source=bl&ots=Sbh8NrXyl-&sig=Vjycklatdf-NACnza4424UVUJ3w&hl=en&sa=X&ei=rN_XVJrMDIHigwTtw4LQDw&ved=0CCYQ6AEwAQ#v=onepage&q=Dr. Eva Snead, San Francisco has one of the highest cancer rates in the country&f=false

[44] http://educate-yourself.org/nwo/reportironmountain2.shtml

[45]	http://www.google.com/url?sa=t&rct=j&q=&esrc=s&source=web&cd=7&ved=0CEwQFjAG&url=http://costsofwar.org/sites/all/themes/costsofwar/images/Civilian_Death.pdf&ei=seDXVJ7IKIWuggSwn4TQAQ&usg=AFQjCNGZ5F1Rgdc64Kmq67NvVhBcrQV0ng

[46] https://thewhiteroseii.wordpress.com/tag/surveillance/

[47] http://en.wikipedia.org/wiki/Paul_E._Vallely

[48] http://en.wikipedia.org/wiki/Temple_of_Set

[49] http://en.wikipedia.org/wiki/BrainGate

[50] http://en.wikipedia.org/wiki/Sanctions_against_Iraq

[51] http://israelect.com/reference/WillieMartin/AIDS.htm

[52] http://all-natural.com/riley.html

[53] http://en.wikisource.org/wiki/Riegle_Report

[54] Forced Sale of Gas Ingredient to Army

[55] http://www.theforbiddenknowledge.com/hardtruth/resnick_inter-view_peter_kawaja.htm

[56] Gulf War Registry

[57] http://en.wikipedia.org/wiki/Oklahoma_City_bombing

[58] https://nwoobserver.wordpress.com/2009/page/70/

[59]http://www.washingtonpost.com/blogs/therootdc/post/ron-paul-dennis-kucinich-wont-soon-be-forgotten/2012/05/15/gIQAgJbzRU_b-log.html

[60]http://rense.com/general79/oldtime.htm

[61]http://www.apfn.org/apfn/camps.htm

[62]http://www.bibliotecapleyades.net/sociopolitica/master_file/youare-foundingfathers.htm

www.ingramcontent.com/pod-product-compliance
Lightning Source LLC
Chambersburg PA
CBHW070005300526
45794CB00001B/191